The
Forgotten Children

Published by

PaperJacks

In association with
ADDICTION RESEARCH FOUNDATION
Toronto
An Agency of the Province of Ontario

Books in this series published by General Publishing Company Limited on behalf of the Addiction Research Foundation of Ontario represent the clinical experience and research findings of a distinguished group of scientists and clinicians serving on the staff of this world renowned research and teaching centre.

The Forgotten Children

A Study of Children

with Alcoholic Parents

by R. Margaret Cork

PaperJacks

A Division of General Publishing Co. Limited, Don Mills

AN ORIGINAL CANADIAN

PaperJacks

One of a series of Canadian books
first published by PaperJacks Ltd.

THE FORGOTTEN CHILDREN

PaperJacks edition published 1969

Reissued June, 1980

Reprinted October, 1982

ISBN 0-7701-0244-1

Foreword

In their concern for the alcoholic, researchers have often overlooked his family. We therefore have little understanding of the sufferings of thousands of children in our communities. The study on which this book is based was concerned with 115 children one or both of whose parents are alcoholic, and the purpose of the book is to promote increased understanding of such children.

The author, Margaret Cork, is a social worker with 15 years' experience as a clinician in the field of alcoholism. Many unanswered questions prompted her to undertake this study. Is the alcoholic solely respons-ible for the breakdown of his family life? Are his children more severely damaged than those in other troubled homes? Is harm to his children related more closely to drinking or to the quality of the relationship between the alcoholic and his wife? Should the family as a whole be treated? Would this produce a more complete recovery for the alcoholic? Would it produce a lower rate of alcoholism, later on, in his children? Where the alcoholic and his wife refuse outside help, is there any way in which assistance can be given separately to their children?

The language of this book has purposely been kept straightforward and non-technical. Although it is basically a research report, it is not intended for a research or specialist audience. Its style, rather, represents an attempt to communicate directly with all who are interested in children – physicians, nurses, psychologists, teachers, social workers, and members of the general public. It is hoped that with increased understanding there may come greater efforts to help those who are, all too often, the forgotten children.

H. David Archibald,
Executive Director,
Addiction Research Foundation,
Toronto.

Contents

Publisher's Note

The United Nations has designated 1979 as International Year of the Child, to foster understanding and promotion of the rights of children all over the world.

When Margaret Cork wrote this book, she was concerned with a particular problem: that of the child with alcoholic parents. However, Miss Cork has devoted her entire career to the rights of children, and she believes that the findings in this book can be applied to children everywhere who are facing problems with little understanding or help from the adult world.

The
Forgotten Children

1.

Two Forgotten Children

"I first remember trouble in our family when I was five," said Jerome, a slight, intelligent looking youngster of twelve. Jerome is the son of a professional man. He is the only boy in a family of three children. When he came into my office Jerome could hardly wait for me to say, "Tell me about the trouble," before he began talking.

"My father mostly starts on a Thursday and drinks until he gets sick," said Jerome. "Then I have to look after him. I bring him a glass of milk and clean things up when he's been sick all over the living room."

Jerome was the third child from an alcoholic home who had been in my office that day, and the tenth that week. As a social worker with a special interest in the children of alcoholics, I had undertaken a study in which I would interview 115 of these children who were between the ages of ten and sixteen in order to learn how they perceived their family life and its effects on them. A cold Toronto rain drizzling down outside was only too appropriate an accompaniment to the stories I had been hearing. I asked Jerome, "Where is your mother when this happens?"

"She's at work and the girls won't clean up, so I have to. It makes me feel awful." Jerome was silent for a few seconds. "The worst times are when Dad hits Mom."

"What do you do?"

"One time when he was hitting her, I ran up and hit him as hard as I could with one of my toys – I don't even remember what it was – and after that it was all a blank. I don't remember what happened. Mostly when he's been drinking just a little he brings me presents. He's easier to get along with than Mom, but when he's drunk he's bad tempered and talks all the time – crazy stuff. He starts in on Mother's family, says they aren't as good as his. I think he wants to hurt her when he's drunk. Maybe he wants to all the time, but he shows it most when he's loaded."

"How does your mother react?"

"She starts yelling back. They just fight all the time."

"Which is worse, the fighting or the drinking?"

"The fighting. Even when I'm in bed I hear it. You can't ever get away from it, but sometimes you have a rest from the drinking."

"How does the fighting make you feel?"

"Mad, and pretty scared." Jerome hung his head.

"Usually I start crying."

I asked what else Jerome could tell me about things at home.

"It's always just the same. Dad goes to work and comes home drunk, or else he brings the stuff home and gets drunk there. I wouldn't mind his drinking if he'd be quiet and leave us alone, but he always seems to want to pick a fight. If Mom goes upstairs to get away, he starts in on us kids."

For a moment Jerome looked dreamily off into space. "Sometimes Dad gets all emotional. He cries. I try to talk to him or Mom does, and he just cries some more. Then she starts and so do I. Sometimes he comes into my room and sits on my bed or lies on it when I'm in bed. He says that Mom doesn't love him, that no one does, or he says he's a lousy father. I get so upset I don't know what to say. I just cry and cry until Mom comes home. I try to push him off the bed, but he just stays there saying all these things."

"Where is your mother when this happens?"

"She's a nurse. She works on the night shift."

"What happens when she gets home?"

"She won't sleep with Dad, then they start to argue. He argues with everything Mom says. Sometimes at night he calls her until she comes to him in the rec room, and it goes on until she stops him."

"How does she do that?"

"They have a fight – a fist fight. I hear them sometimes. I come down from my room and start to fight with Dad too, but it doesn't do any good. He still hits her. She just takes it and tells me to go back to bed, but I can't go to sleep. You just feel hopeless."

"How is your father when he's sober?"

"Mostly when he's sober he's away at work or he's sleeping or finding fault. He talks a lot but he never remembers what he says. He acts as though things never happened. It's like he loses his memory."

"What sort of things does he say?"

"Things like telling Mother he should have dropped her eight or nine years ago."

"Can you talk to him when he's sober?"

"No. Usually I'm in bed when he comes home." Jerome paused. "Sometimes when he's sober he's like a father should be."

"How is that?"

"When he's sober he's so nice that I wish he'd drink all the time."

"Why?"

"Sometimes I wish he'd be one or the other. I don't really know him. Fathers shouldn't drink."

"Do you talk to your mother?"

"No. I don't talk to any of them. Mostly we all fight or are mad at each other."

I asked who took care of the house, who got the meals, who did the washing and housework.

"Mostly the house is a mess. My sister does some. Sometimes if Dad isn't drinking he comes home and gets a meal. Then he goes up to his study and works. Sometimes we go to school in dirty clothes because Mom's too tired to do the washing." Jerome looked down at his clothes, which were of good quality but far from clean. "She's not going to work because of bringing me here, so I guess she'll do a washing to-night."

"How do you feel about your mother working?"

"It's better, I guess. More money, not so many

worries. But I don't like being alone with Dad. And I wish Mom wasn't always so tired and mad."

"How does your mother feel about the drinking?"

"She hates it. She tries to stop him from drinking, but she seems mad at him even when he isn't."

"How do your sisters react when your father is drinking?"

"They get really upset, and the little one starts howling her head off. They get over it, but I don't. I can't do anything. Do you understand? *I can't do anything*," he repeated, very loudly. Then in his usual tone of voice, "I used to be on Dad's side, then I was on both – one minute on hers and the next on Dad's."

I asked what he meant by being on Dad's side.

"Well, he's an alcoholic and he has to drink. He can't ever stop. Still, I guess Mom has to take a lot and when I realize that, I'm on her side. Sometimes I wish she'd let him keep right on drinking and then he'd finish himself off."

At this point Jerome got up and started pacing up and down the room. "Sometimes he goes away for days. He says he has business out of town, but I think he doesn't want to face things. Then he comes back and says he'll never do it again. It's not exactly breaking his word, because he can't help it. But Mom doesn't seem to understand that. I used to just let her nag at him but now I start talking back to her. I guess I do things to make her mad, but I can't seem to help it."

"How does your mother take it?"

"She doesn't like it, but she can't do anything about it – neither of them can. If they're going to act that way, so am I."

"Who does the disciplining around the house?"

"Nobody. They try but then they forget about it, so we all just do what we like. Nobody tells you what to do, then they get mad at you for doing something on your own."

"Tell me how your parents are when your father isn't drinking. Do they have fun together or go places?"

"No. They're always mad at each other, and they haven't any friends. This summer things really got worse, and Mom said she'd leave again. She's done that three times. She goes to our lawyer when she can't take any more, and then either we leave or Dad does."

"How are things when your parents are separated?"

"Better. The house is peaceful and Mom isn't so upset, not so bad tempered."

"Why do you think your parents go back together?"

"Well, I think Mother thinks Dad needs her, and he promises not to drink any more. He gives her money and she gets soft and lets him come back. He's fine for a week or so, then he starts in again. She should know he'll never keep his promises."

"How do you feel when your father is away?"

"I don't really want them to separate. I'd rather have a father even if he drinks. The kids all know why he isn't there. They laugh at me, and I don't want to go to school."

"How is school going?"

"I'm always at the bottom of the class. It makes you feel dumb."

"Why do you think you're having trouble at school?"

"I can't think about things properly. I never have any peace to do my homework. I can't stop thinking about how things will be when I get home."

"Do you belong to any after-school clubs?"

"No, I just fool around – mostly watch TV. Sometimes I play solitaire or have a game of cards with my little sister, but we're mostly all mad at each other." After a long pause Jerome added, "My sisters call me a cry baby."

"What about your friends?"

"I don't really know anyone. I don't think the kids like me much."

"Why not?"

"Well, they ask me to do things with them, and my eyes are all red from crying and I won't let them see me, so I mostly just say I can't go. Mostly I'm by myself – there isn't anyone I really know. We've moved a lot and I don't want to make new friends. Even if I had a friend, I wouldn't bring him home. I wouldn't want him to know what my family is like."

"Why not?"

"I'm afraid he'd hear the fighting or see my Dad, and then he wouldn't like me."

"Did you ever tell any of the kids how things are at home?"

"No, Mom says we shouldn't tell anyone. Anyway, I'd hate for them to know."

"How about telling one of your teachers?"

"No."

"Why not?"

"You're too ashamed. They might fail you or pick on you. People shouldn't know your business. I wouldn't want them to feel sorry for me."

Abruptly Jerome said, "It's too late for us."

"Too late?"

"Yes. He'll never stop drinking. Ours is no good of

a family, but you just have to take it until you can get away from them."

"Do you ever do things together as a family?"

"When I was very little we used to go on picnics. Now sometimes we go to a show, but it's never any fun because we always end up fighting."

"How do you think a family should be?"

"Do things together, get along, have some fun. You should be able to like your parents. Everything in our house is just to keep Dad from being upset. If my sisters and me try to have some fun, Mom tells us to be quiet so Dad can sleep it off or so he won't get worked up."

"How is your mother when he isn't drinking?"

"Well, always so tired and worried about money."

"Doesn't Dad support you?"

"Well I know he could, but all he makes goes into drinking or paying off his debts, and Mom has to work to pay some of them. I hate him for this, because I know he's a clever person who could look after us if he didn't act the way he does. I wish Mom would stand up to him and make him. You can't really talk to Mom about this or anything. She just talks about her worries, never seems to care about yours. She's always just thinking of ways to make him stop or how she can keep the house going when there's never any money. She never pays attention to anyone but my Dad. She tells me not to worry, but I do."

"What do you worry about?"

"About what will happen. They're not like other parents."

"How are other parents, do you think?"

"They pay some attention to their kids. They really know what goes on. We all get away with anything and they don't care. Suppose I'm away from school – I just write a note and she signs it. Say we're all fighting – they never bother to find out what the trouble really is. They don't know what's happening to you. You feel sort of alone."

"How do you think things will be in the future?"

"Well, if Mom and Dad separate, things might be okay. But I don't think Mom will ever stick to it, so it's hopeless to think they'll be any different. I'll just go away somewhere when I'm old enough and forget the lot of them. Families aren't much good to you."

"Will you have a family when you grow up?"

"Never. I might make a mess of it too, and I'd never wish that on any kid. I don't feel like other kids who have a normal family – nearly failing at school, no friends, no one to talk to. They're all a bunch of nuts – I don't care about any of them – Mom, Dad, my sisters, school, everybody."

I asked Jerome what he would do about drinking when he was old enough to drink.

"I don't think I'll ever touch it. I might get to be like Dad. But then, everybody we know takes a drink or two, so I might. But not like Dad does."

"Do you ever try to tell your father how you feel about his drinking?"

"He'd just be madder. I sometimes think if Mom didn't get so mad, say such mean things to him, he might not drink as much. But she can't seem to stop yakking any more than he can stop drinking. Once I asked him why he drank. I told him I was ashamed of him."

"What did he say?"

"He said he couldn't help it."

"How did you feel?"

"I just felt sorry for him. I guess I knew he couldn't help it, but I still felt ashamed of him."

Finally, I asked Jerome how he would describe alcoholism.

"It's somebody that has a problem," he said, "like my Dad not being happy in childhood. Alcoholics don't want to think of anything but themselves, or they want to forget something. It's like there's a door and they won't open it because they're afraid, so they drink." Jerome paused. "Sometimes it's like he's not there."

"Not there?"

"Well, he asks you to do things with him, but it's always things he wants to do. You can't ask him to do things you want."

"Why not?"

"Well, Mom says just to go along with him whatever he wants, and I do it, but it's not like other parents. It's like my parents don't care whether you're there or not. I'm always afraid to be natural. I always have to stop and think how they'll be, whether what I say or do is going to upset them. You feel like you're not a child, like you have to watch yourself. You feel like you're more grown up than they are."

There is little need to highlight Jerome's sense of deprivation and insecurity. The home situation he described seemed to leave him filled with conflict, resentment, anxiety, and anger. He appeared to be torn between passively accepting the situation and expressing his anger inappropriately in tears, at times even wishing that his father "would finish himself off." Because his home life seemed to provide few standards of behavior, little or no discipline or guidance, Jerome is left feeling confused, unsure of himself, and uncertain of his role in the family. He has tried desperately to understand and to reach his father, but he has been rewarded only by tremendous emotional demands which a boy cannot meet and which leave him anxious and upset. It is particularly difficult and frustrating for him to see his mother hurt by his father and to feel powerless to stop it. This boy has had no good male model on which to pattern himself. His mother's escape in words, her inability to take any realistic action, and her need to work and to leave the boy alone with his drinking parent seem to have reinforced his loneliness and sense of being unloved. His mother's seeming inability to understand and to care for him have left Jerome as hostile toward her as toward his father.

As well as being deprived of love, support, and approval from his parents, Jerome has a sense of being somewhat neglected physically. He says he is ridiculed by his parents for crying so much, yet receives little or no help in dealing with this symptom of his anxiety. From his brothers and sisters and neighborhood children he gains none of the support and approval so vital to normal growing up. It is not hard to understand why this boy has little self-esteem, nor to see how his absorption in his own problems may leave him almost no chance to develop a sense of responsibility or ability to face life's problems.

All too early Jerome has become aware of an adult world in which people seem to hurt one another and refuse to face their responsibilities. As a result, it is hard to see how he can enter adulthood as a responsible, loving human being or how, if he marries, he can make a life for his children which is much better than his own.

So much for one forgotten child. He is much like most of the 114 others who were interviewed, although many appeared to be more severely damaged. To demonstrate this similarity and to present the situation from a girl's viewpoint, however, it might be well to look at some excerpts from my conversation with Sally, a fourteen-year-old whom I also regard as typical.

Sally is the second of five children, three of whom were interviewed in the course of this study. She was brought to my office by her mother. All the other children were also in the car because it was a Friday and their father had already begun his weekend drinking. Although the father's earning capacity was high, the children were all rather poorly dressed. Sally had a particularly neglected appearance and very poor posture. Her face seemed strained and her expression lifeless.

Sally began the interview by saying, "I always feel sad, not just because my father drinks but because of the way he is." Then she burst into tears. When she had pulled herself together, she added somewhat bitterly, "He's always getting mad and smashing things. Once when I was little he came home late. Mother hadn't kept his supper hot so he tipped up the table with everything on it. You can never forget those times."

"What does your mother do?" I asked.

"She yells and nags. She's always nagging, but he drinks and acts like that anyway. Anything can start him off, but mostly it's Mom. Pretty soon he's yelling at all of us. He never wants to eat with us – just lies around and moans and groans, saying how awful he feels. It never stops until he falls asleep. Sometimes he wakes up in the middle of the night yelling for one of us to bring him a drink of water."

"What do you do?"

"Bring it to him. We all do what he wants so he won't start another fight. He makes us do whatever he wants, and she makes us too. If everybody does what he wants, then things go better. But things are always up and down."

"How does all this make you feel?"

"I keep wishing he'd just drink like other people. But the nagging and the fighting are worse than the alcohol. He hits Mom sometimes."

"Do you ever tell your father how you feel?"

"No."

"Why not?"

"He'd hurt you – say mean things. You just can't talk to him about anything that matters."

"How do you feel about the way your mother and father get along?"

"I hate him, but sometimes I think Mom asks for it. She gets him going until he starts to drink."

"Do they ever do things together, such as going out with friends or bowling?"

"Sometimes Mom goes out to a dinner with Dad, but mostly he doesn't ask her. If she goes, I think she does it just to see that he doesn't drink too much. She never acts as though they had a good time. They're always fighting and arguing by the time they get home. They never really have any fun."

"Does your mother do things by herself, like visiting with neighbors or friends?"

"No, she never talks to the neighbors and hasn't any friends."

"Does your father help your mother around the house?"

"No, he's always sleeping it off or fighting. Mom has to do everything, or else we try to do it. There's never any time for fun. Mom used to try to get help in the house, but she never has the money to pay anyone so she's stopped. Nobody seems to care what happens."

"Do you all have special jobs to do?"

"No. Mom just yells at whoever is nearest. We never know what we're supposed to do, and then she gets mad because we don't do things."

"Do your mother and father ever make plans for holidays or special occasions?"

"Never. They just argue. Things just happen in our house. You never know what's what."

After a pause Sally continued, "My father thinks we all hate him."

"Is he right?"

"When he talks like that I feel awful because I don't want to hate him. I try to understand that he's sick, but sometimes I think he drinks because he doesn't like us."

"Do you like him?"

"Yes and no. Sometimes I feel sorry for him, and then again I get so mad I hate him – I hate both of them. They're not happy and neither are we, even when he isn't drinking. We kids all fight just like Mom and Dad. You can't get away from it unless you leave."

"Do you think you'll leave?"

"Yes, as soon as I'm sixteen. But that's a long time off. I don't know how I can take it that long."

I asked Sally how well her father supported the family.

"He's a really great salesman," she replied, "so he should be able to. Last month he got a thousand-dollar bonus. He gave Mother money for groceries, but she never saw any of the rest of it. He gave it away or drank it, I guess. He never really supports us properly, and this makes Mom mad. I sort of think Dad holds out on Mom just to make her mad or to punish her. But I understand how he hates her to be at him. She's always at us too. She doesn't see we feel the same way."

Sally continued talking about her father. "Sometimes Dad goes out and buys us clothes, but he never asks Mother or us what we really need or want. It's just his way of playing the big shot, as though he was trying to buy us. I think he's trying to be nice to us – Mom doesn't even try – but you never know how he'll be. For instance, at Christmas he knows we want special things but he figures Mother will get them and he doesn't need to, so he drinks all his money or gives it away. He drives people all over the city and entertains them. He spends more time and money on them than us. It's as though he wants people to like him but he doesn't know how to be normal. It makes me feel pretty left out and sort of hopeless."

"Do you ever talk to your mother about how you feel?"

"You can't talk to her because she doesn't pay any attention to you. She just worries about Dad. He's sometimes understanding when he's sober, but she never even told me about the facts of life. I asked her, but she wouldn't talk about it. She doesn't care what we do as long as we don't upset Dad."

"Tell me about your friends. Do they know how things are?"

"No, I never bring them around when Mom and Dad are fighting. When I do bring friends in, he's always so nice to them that they think he's swell. He's nice to everyone but his family." Here Sally burst into tears again. "I don't ever want the other kids to know."

"Why not?"

"They might not like me. I'd be so ashamed for them to know how we all fight."

"Do you ever talk to any other adults? Perhaps to an aunt or your minister or a teacher, about how things are at home?"

"No, Mom says to keep it in the family. Anyway, what could they do? They wouldn't understand, and then they'd know and I'd feel worse. I wouldn't be able to face them."

After a pause Sally added, "I feel different from other kids. Of course, we might be more like other families if Dad didn't throw his money away. We could have things and do things like other kids. I know Dad really could afford to send me to university, but when the time comes I suppose he won't have the money. Anyway, I'd never be able to concentrate enough."

It is not difficult to see from Sally's words just how negative and inadequate a relationship she feels her parents have with each other. There is not only constant verbal abuse but violence as well. This relationship is far harder for Sally to understand and accept than the excessive drinking. There is no sharing between them concerning the care of the home or the children. There are no jointly planned family activities. Her parents seem to be isolated from other adults and adult experiences. Even the occasional night out at a company dinner is not a source of genuine pleasure. While her father relates to others, he seems to do so in a way which only serves to increase Sally's anger and sense of rejection.

Since she sees her parents as having little capacity to love one another, it is not surprising that Sally does not feel close to either of them. She believes that because of their absorption in themselves and their own suffering, both are unaware of her problems and of her identity as an important member of the family. When she tries to reach them, it is only at the cost of further rejection. It is obvious that she feels conflict concerning their behavior toward her and one another as well as about her feelings for them, particularly her feelings toward her father. She has some insight into his behavior but very little into her mother's. At times she seems to be trying to excuse her father's behavior on the basis that he is sick, but she is unable to make any allowances for her mother's. In fact, she tends to blame her mother for some of the things her father does.

Sally is filled with anger and takes out some of it on her brothers and sisters. She is consumed with a sense of hopelessness. Her only means of coping with it is to dream of escape.

Sally expressed the feeling that she didn't really know her parents. She admitted that they took care of her physically to some extent, but she indicated that their behavior in other ways fell far short of that of other parents. She said that she feels isolated from her parents and insecure in her relationships with other adults; even with her friends Sally experiences considerable shame and a deep fear that she will not be liked. It is not hard to see what effect this may have on future relationships.

If more of Sally's story were presented, we would see even more evidence of its similarity to Jerome's – for example, her failures at school and her inability to find satisfying interests or hobbies. Neither Sally nor Jerome seems to have had much opportunity within the family for healthy growth. Both expressed feelings of insecurity, confusion, frustration, anger, rejection, and isolation. Both seem depressed about the future. It is particularly alarming to note in each of them many of the characteristics often found in alcoholics.

2.

Who are the Forgotten Children?

"It's too late to make things different for me, but if somebody understands how awful it really is, maybe they will help some other kids." These are the words of Peter, who is fifteen, and they illustrate the plight of many children of alcoholic parents. In the first chapter, we listened closely to two of them. It is time, now, to take a look at my group of 115 children as a whole.

Considerable research into the causes of alcoholism has been carried out over the past few decades. Great efforts have also been made to treat alcoholism. But only in comparatively recent years have we begun to study the families of alcoholics. At all levels of research and treatment, their children have been grossly neglected. By talking with them, I hoped to gain new insight into the alcoholic and his mate as well as a deeper understanding of the effects of their home life on their children.*

One of the most surprising aspects of this study was the whole-hearted response of the children in spite of their natural shyness and tension. These anxieties showed up in unwillingness to remove a coat, sitting on the edge of a chair, twisting a cap into a ball, clasping and unclasping hands, or wandering around the room. A few cried during the interview, but this seemed related to the subjects discussed rather than to anxiety about taking part. With some, of course, it may have been a bit of both. With most, signs of defensiveness about the interview decreased or disappeared as it progressed.

A few of the ten-year-olds initially found it harder than the older children to put their feelings into words. These children needed a little more support from me, but they too became visibly more relaxed and more eloquent after a while. Nearly all the children seemed to gain satisfaction and a sense of release from talking to someone about a subject that was usually taboo. In fact, most wanted to talk longer than the prescribed half to three-quarters of an hour, and a good many talked as though a dam had burst. A very few seemed strained throughout the interview and relieved when the time was up, but none showed any inclination to leave early.

Until now, most research on families of alcoholics has been focussed on those in the lower socio-economic

---

*Details concerning the procedures used in this study may be found in the Appendix.

group. Very little attention has been paid to those in the middle or upper socio-economic levels. It is important to keep in mind that the children who took part in this study came from a wide variety of socio-economic groups.** People cling to the idea that alcoholism seldom affects family life except at the lower socio-economic levels, and it is all too easy to assume from the children's words that the feelings they expressed and the experiences they reported will only be found at these levels. In actual fact, a majority of the children in this study came from middle or upper class families.

All of the children, except one sixteen-year-old dropout, were attending school. All except the children of the eight couples who were separated lived at home with both parents. While no psychological testing was done on the children, all but two responded to questions in ways that suggested normal or above normal intelligence. Although 53 had failed a grade, most of the rest were doing more-or-less average school work for their age. Most of the children had a parent or parents who were still drinking, but 15 had parents who had been abstinent for periods varying from one to five years. These children were asked to talk about their reactions and feelings during the pre-recovery period and were all of an age to recall this vividly.

As to age and sex, the children were a fairly representative group.

** Their fathers ranged from laborers to skilled workers to professionals. Fathers' education ranged from a few years of elementary school to university graduation.

TABLE I
NUMBER OF CHILDREN BY AGE AND SEX

Age	Male	Female	Total
10	5	13	18
11	11	6	17
12	9	5	14
13	10	4	14
14	9	7	16
15	9	12	21
16	6	9	15
Total	59	56	115

The foregoing represents rather superficial information about the children who took part in this study. More important was the insight I gained into their relationships with other children, with brothers and sisters, their school life, and the place of fun and recreation in their lives.

I don't go places with my friends and their parents because I can't ever take my friends places.

While the majority of these children said they had playmates or acquaintances, only a very few told of friendships in which they felt secure enough to share their troubles. In the average family, children show some reticence in discussing family affairs with others. Where a parent's behavior seems to them to reflect on their own worth, they tend to hide that behavior. Nevertheless, the children in most healthy families have at least one close friend with whom they feel free to talk frankly and openly about their parents' idiosyncrasies. By contrast, most of the children in my study tended to try to hide nearly all parental behavior from other children. Thus, their friendships were not as deep as they might otherwise have been.

A few children, particularly the younger ones,*** said that they occasionally brought friends into their homes, but most said they did not because they were afraid their friends would witness parental drinking or fighting. While some spent considerable time in the homes of their friends, this often seemed only to heighten their internal conflict and increase their sense of being different. As a result, most of the children habitually played in the streets.

A large number, particularly those in the middle and older groups, described themselves as being uncomfortable with their friends because they could not uphold their own end of a friendship. "I always feel like I'm a phoney – hiding something from them." Others said they could not make friends at all because of the fear that people would find out "what our family is like" or think "that I'm as crazy as my parents."

The older children seemed to have particular difficulties in making and keeping friends. A few had tried, but their friends had been subjected to ridicule or insults on visits to the children's homes. Others said they had no time for friends because they were burdened with household responsibilities. One child said she was

---

***Since the children interviewed represented a wide age range, I found it convenient to divide them into three groups: *the younger group* (10–11), *the middle group* (12–14), and *the older group* (15–16).

friendless because she was not allowed normal freedom. Another said, "Dad gives me so many things and I boast about them, so no one likes me."

Thus we see that at a period in their lives when most youngsters are forming and consolidating friendships, most of the children in this study seemed to have relationships that were limited by insecurity, fear, and lack of trust. At a time when they most needed to be liked, many were deprived of this necessity. By contrast, they were learning to be wary of others and to hold back normal expressions of affection. For most of these children there was little of the companionship that experts believe is so vital to healthy growth and the formation of secure relationships later.

Everybody at our house is angry all the time.

The children's relationships with their brothers and sisters appeared to be characterized by considerable tension and competition. This was not the sort of rivalry that is part of normal family life. Instead, it was the same kind of fighting that their parents indulged in – the kind that seems to result in progressive damage to all family members.

A few of the younger children (ages ten and eleven) said they had relatively close relationships with older brothers or sisters who gave them care and attention. "My brother really likes me and is interested in me," said one boy. "My sister takes care of me like a mother should," said another. But even in these households the children fought and quarrelled among themselves more than is normal. At the same time, a number of younger children resented the parental role assumed by the older ones. "He just tries to boss me," commented one. "She's not my mother, so why should I mind her?" demanded another. While this problem occurs to some extent in normal families, parents usually keep it under control. With some of the older children in my study, the apparent need to dominate their juniors was probably a result of deep feelings of aggression or frustration.

Those in the middle group (ages twelve to fourteen) seemed to be even more caught up in destructive rivalries within the family. They were more than normally sensitive to parental favoring of younger children. "The little ones get all the attention," and "They only like you when you're little," are typical statements. Many said they were constantly urged to side with one parent or the other. The children often felt that this separated them from one another. Many were upset because "everyone in our house goes his own way," and because rules that applied to them did not apply to the younger ones. At the same time, they were often fearful of standing up to their parents in the way that some of their older brothers and sisters did. The middle child in any family may tend to feel isolated, but those in this study seemed to suffer from this feeling more than most.

Among the older children (ages fifteen and sixteen), I saw a wide variation in their feelings about younger brothers and sisters. About a third said they felt an unusual degree of responsibility toward the younger ones — not only for their physical care, but also for their emotional development. Many tried, without much success, to prepare the younger children for the problems they themselves were facing. The rest accepted their responsibilities with resentment. "I'm sick of looking after kids," they said, or "I feel like I've been a mother already and I'm only fifteen."

Thus we see that in all age groups there appeared to be an abnormal amount of dissension and separation among brothers and sisters. Generally there was little or no basic warmth and affection; instead, there was a deep sense of hostility and resentment. The words of one child are particularly revealing: "We all just go off and nurse our wounds – nobody cares how you feel."

There was a keen awareness of family disunity. Because of their isolation from friends, brothers and sisters were thrown back on each other; yet they seemed pathetically limited in their ability to give each other warmth and understanding.

I worry all afternoon at school about how things will be when I get home.

Many of the younger children in my study liked school and were doing relatively well in it. This did not appear to be primarily because of interest in school work, though a few enjoyed it. Rather, it seemed to be because school was a place where these children found peace: "You can stop thinking about things at home when you're at school." A good many, however, made very different statements: "I'm at the bottom of the class because I can't think properly when Dad's that way." One youngster spoke of missing a lot of school because "I have such nightmares, my nerves are bad."

Many in the middle group of children had begun to fail in school. "I just wasn't going to try if they wouldn't act decently," or "I got behind because I was sick whenever the fighting was worst," or "Dad played the hi-fi so loud every night I couldn't study." Even some of those who were not failing expressed difficulty in concentrating. For them, school was something to be endured. It highlighted their sense of inadequacy.

According to the older children, school was beginning to present much more serious problems. Here there were more failures of one or even two grades. There were also more thwarted ambitions. Some said they couldn't face years of having to study under unfavorable circumstances. Some stated that parental drinking would use up the money that would otherwise have sent them to college. Others had lost interest in school because they felt a need to go to work and help out. "Father spends it all on drink."

Only a few children expressed hopes of going on to university. For most, school held little sense of adventure or achievement. Few of the children who did well in school seemed to receive recognition at home; those who did poorly were castigated or belittled by their parents. Competition with their schoolmates offered little enjoyment for these children because they felt inferior to or isolated from them.

The kids at school all talk about the fun they have with their families. It makes me feel sort of left out.

Nearly all of the children lamented the lack of fun in their lives, and few took part in group play. A few of the younger ones said, "Dad's sometimes fun when he's sober or even when he's drinking." More typical was: "He plays with you, but only when you're little. Mom's never any fun." Many of the children compared their homes with others in which the parents "fool with their kids and have fun." Most said their homes lacked opportunity for fun. "We don't even own a pack of cards," said one. "If we play games with Dad, he always has to win or he gets mad," or "All the others in my class can still laugh at funny things but I can't." Thus it was evident that the children in all age groups had little or no opportunity for the fun and laughter that is essential to childhood and to the growth of personality.

Only a small proportion of the children in my study were involved in community activities. For those who were, the purpose was apparently to escape from home rather than to learn or to make new friends. None said they had a close relationship with other children involved in the same community group. None indicated that they really knew the leaders, with the exception of one sixteen-year-old boy who said his camp director was "like a father to me." Most spoke like fifteen-year-old Susan. "What good is judo to me when I haven't any friends? The gym is just a place to get away from home."

As I reviewed my data, it became evident that nearly half the children had some special difficulty that complicated the picture. In 28 cases, the child had an alcoholic mother rather than an alcoholic father; in ten cases, the child had two alcoholic parents. Fourteen children had parents who were separated. Eight children had no brothers or sisters. I found myself wondering whether the children in these special categories suffered more than the others or in ways that were different.

I feel worse because there's just me.

The only child has long been a subject for speculation. Every child is affected by his position in the family – whether he is the oldest, the youngest, a middle child, or an only child. Relationships with parents are probably a more important influence on personality development than the presence or absence of brothers and sisters, but some psychologists believe that having other children in the family helps a child to learn to get along with other people and to develop a healthy personality.

Perhaps the words of some of the children who took part in this study can help us to understand the feelings of the only child in an alcholic's family. A boy of ten: "There never was anyone; I felt so lonely." A boy of fourteen: "They spoil me when they're drinking, give me anything I want; then when they're not drinking or fighting, they ignore me."

The words of other only children also express this feeling of loneliness: "I'm just on my own – there's nobody at home after school because Mom goes to work," or "When Dad was drinking Mom would be far away like, so you felt alone." An adolescent girl, looking back, remarked: "I always had to take sides and I would get all mixed up. Perhaps if I hadn't been an only child, I wouldn't have minded so much. I was in

the middle all the time, and I didn't know whose side
to be on."

It seems obvious that an only child in an alcoholic
family situation will feel especially isolated. He must
face his parents' drinking and quarrelling alone. He has
no one in the family from whom to obtain even frag-
ments of emotional satisfaction or on whom he can
drain off some of his hostility. While the majority of
the children I talked with said they did not discuss their
problems with brothers and sisters and did not feel
close to them, the mere fact of having a brother or sister
must surely have lessened their sense of isolation. In
ordinary situations an only child tends to become more
egocentric than a child who has brothers and sisters; in
the home of an alcoholic, it seems likely that this
characteristic will become accentuated.

*I can take it when one of them drinks, but I really
get scared when they both start.*

The child who has both parents alcoholic has a
special set of problems. One twelve-year-old said,
"They take turns – so it's always there." An older child
remarked, "Father tries to stop but Mom begs him for
a drink, so he gets fed up and gets the stuff for both of
them. You'd think they'd help each other stop, but it's
the other way around." Several children in this situation
said they felt grossly burdened by responsibility: "I
feel like I'm the mother and the father. There's no one
who cares what happens – they both just ignore us."

Some of the children who were seen at a time when
one parent had attained sobriety said with great
vehemence, "He could stop if she did," or "She could

stop if she cared enough." Apparently they identified more with the parent who had achieved sobriety than with the one who had not. However, few of them felt really close to either parent, drinking or sober.

It is fairly clear that the child of two alcoholics suffers doubly. For him there are few intervals of parental sobriety. The children of two alcoholics have no one on whom to depend for the normal running of the home, the preparation of meals, or the care of clothing, let alone parental guidance and stability.

Mom doesn't look after us. I have to be the mother myself.

Most of the children whose mothers were alcoholic said that mothers – or women in general – should not drink. Even those children who said, "It's all right for Dad to drink," felt that mother's drinking was "disgusting – not like a mother." Much of their concern was centered around her inability to look after them. This was particularly true of the younger group. Older children said things like, "I feel like I have to be the mother because Mom's so wrapped up in herself."

Many more were concerned about their mothers' lack of interest in them and their inability to relate to her. One said, "I wouldn't mind her drinking if I could just be noticed." Another asked, "I like her, but does she like me?" Said a third, "I haven't missed her because I never really knew her. When she was drinking she was a person you could never reach." Said a fourth, "She still ignores us even though she's sober."

Approximately equal numbers of boys and girls expressed doubts about marriage for themselves, but where the father was the alcoholic more girls than boys expressed these doubts and where the mother was the alcoholic more boys spoke of them. The remarks that follow are from children whose mothers were alcoholics. One boy said, "I'm not going to get married. It would be awful to get yourself tied to a woman who drinks." Another boy said, "I'd leave my wife if she drank. It just messes things up for the kids." A girl said, "I don't think I'll have a family; it might be a mess like ours is." Another girl said, "I'd rather have a career; I've had enough of looking after a family." Still another remarked, "I'm cold, just like Dad says Mom is." Their reaction on the whole was one of disgust and shame, though one girl felt her mother talked to her because it was impossible for her mother to talk to her husband: "She sort of depends on me." A few identified with the mother's drinking. One girl said, "My father would drive any woman to drink."

When we realize that most children are close to their mothers, especially during the formative years, it is easy to understand why children whose mothers were alcoholic would feel even more rejected than did the children in the rest of the group – although the non-alcoholic mothers were also found wanting. In addition, most children with alcoholic mothers found their fathers "too busy to pay any attention to us."

It's better with Dad gone, but Mom does seem lonely. I wonder how Dad manages on his own.

Most of the children whose parents were separated expressed the feeling that things were slightly better when the alcoholic parent was out of the home. "Mom's better with him away," said one child. "Dad doesn't get so upset now she's gone," said another. Although many said they did not really know their separated parent or did not miss him, most expressed some longing for their father or, in one case, their mother; and most showed some degree of conflict about the separation. Excerpts from the interviews illustrate some of their mixed feelings:

"It's best for him to be away, even though I'd still like him if he wasn't."

"I like him better than Mom but I don't want him home."

"First I wanted to go with my Dad, then when something happened, I wanted to stay with Mother."

"We have a good housekeeper now Mom's gone, but it's not the same."

"Inside you'll always be different, even though you have adjusted."

Almost all the children described the separated alcoholic parent as a person who was not what a father or a mother should be. They obviously resented this. One described her father as "an unnatural parent, irresponsible and selfish. He is just a fool who runs away from everything – he'd be better off if he dropped dead." Of a separated mother another said, "She's friendly enough, but she acts phoney so you don't even know what to say to her when you go to see her."

About a third of these children said they felt closer to their mothers following the separation. Their family lives were still far from normal, but they had improved: "There's not as much fighting. Mom's not so scared any more; she's more human now. She always used to be on edge; now she laughs and we sometimes enjoy each other. Now I feel more secure – I felt completely lost until he left."

In a family in which the alcoholic mother had left the home, a child said, "Things are better now she's away, and sometimes Dad acts like a real father."

However, two thirds of the children expressed the feeling that even though things were somewhat better, they still did not feel secure or close to the remaining parent. Their words are very revealing: "Mother's still upset. She thinks of her own troubles more than ours. She still seems to care more about Dad than us. Sometimes she doesn't even get our meals or take care of us. We're just a burden to her – we're still not a family."

Some children appeared to resent their parents' separations. Others expressed the feeling that if they hadn't been around, their parents' marriages might have been successful. Still others showed concern for the parent who had left: "Mother seems so awfully lonely." "How will Dad manage on his own?"

Seven of the fourteen children whose parents were separated expressed doubts about marriage for themselves. One said, "If I had been Mom, I'd have left Dad before it made us all a mess. I'll never marry." Another said, "Marriage is too difficult. You might separate and then no one's happy."

While only 14 children had experienced separation, several times this number seemed to live in fear of separation.

"I hope it never happens. We wouldn't know who to go with."

"It would be worse because everyone would know."

"Dad needs someone to look after him."

Many, on the other hand, felt strongly that their parents should separate instead of just threatening to do so.

How can you grow up when they still treat you like a child?

Since so many children in this study were adolescents, it seemed important to examine their responses to problems typical of adolescence. To what extent do the feelings, attitudes, and experiences of the adolescents in this study reflect those of the average adolescent? To what extent do they differ?

For the average child, adolescence is a turbulent time – physically, mentally, and emotionally. It is the time when the child begins the struggle to free himself from his parents. He begins to find out who he is and to gain new feelings of self-esteem. He begins to make decisions for himself and to control his own environment. Very gradually he learns to withstand frustration and to postpone gratification. Slowly he becomes more aware of the world around him and begins to assume new responsibilities. He begins to develop ambitions and to set goals for himself.

During adolescence the young person accepts new ideas and questions old ones. He discovers new ways of using his leisure time. He develops an interest in the opposite sex and transfers some of his dependence from parents to classmates and to adults other than his parents. He makes new social and emotional adjustments. He begins to formulate a set of values and a personal philosophy.

Adolescence brings with it various degrees of conflict, anxiety, and insecurity. A youngster may experience wide mood swings. At times he wants to be alone to daydream about his future. At the same time he wants to have a sense of belonging, both to his family and to groups of young people. He may resent criticism, fearing rejection; he may be openly critical of his home or his parents, comparing them unfavorably with other homes and parents. At times he may be aggressive, strongly competitive, and quarrelsome. However, if his relationships with his parents have been satisfying during earlier years, the average adolescent will have a basic faith and a belief in his parents' love which will carry him through these difficult years. If put to the test, he will acknowledge that he cares for his parents and would not exchange his family for any other.

It is obvious that parents are an important factor in the success with which a child works his way through adolescence. One authority has said that "in the give and take of his relationships with his parents and others, the child finds a sense of security, self-esteem and an ability to deal with complex inner problems he is facing."[1] Says another:

> Parents are models whether they want to be or not....
> While the child is growing away from his parents he
> must still feel the support and strength of ... being a
> completely accepted member of that family.... He needs
> and wants wise limits, encouragement to grow up and to
> test himself in new experiences and relationships.[2]

The words of one of the children in this study are startling when contrasted with this ideal: "They make you feel you're just somebody to boss around, even though you're old enough to look after the little kids for them. I know I should lose weight, but how can you try when they don't try to be different? I want to be somebody but I feel like a nobody. I used to think I could be a teacher but now I know it's hopeless to try."

Few of the children in this study seem to have developed strong emotional ties with their parents. Thus they have no opportunity to experience the normal process of breaking away from parents. The sentiments of many are echoed in these comments:

"They make you feel you're a burden and that they'd be better off without you. We've never mattered to them except to do what they wanted us to do. Sometimes I think they love us, but I'm never sure."

Jersild, the well known child psychologist, says:

> The lot of adolescents who are unloved or rejected by their parents is a hard one ... unless they can find a substitute parent or crumbs of affection outside the home.... Most children who experience this fail to grow normally through adolescence into adulthood. They tend to develop symptoms which may be severe enough to keep them at a preadolescent level of behavior for the rest of their lives.[3]

At the same time, many children in my study expressed the feeling that they had not experienced a normal childhood.

"I grew up and realized about problems awfully fast."

"I can remember feeling more grown up than most of my friends, even when I was little."

"Both of my parents lean on me. Mom made me feel I had to act grown up even when I was quite small."

"No one ever laughs in our house. They never play with us."

"If things had been different, you could have had a childhood."

In addition to their difficulties at home, most of the adolescents in my study seemed to meet frustration at school. Along with a sense of academic inadequacy, many of the children I studied experienced a feeling of separation from their fellow-students. They appeared to have little of the prestige and popularity that are important to the adolescent. Because the alcoholic's family moves so often, many of the youngsters had been forced countless times to make an adjustment to a new school and new classmates and to the children in a new neighborhood. As a result, some children seemed to have given up the struggle; they had stopped trying to adjust and had become friendless.

A few of the children I talked with had normal ambitions: they dreamed about the future as most adolescents do. Unfortunately, unless they have help, their chances of realizing their dreams are exceedingly slight. Most of the children in the study appeared to have realized this: they seemed to have little ambition and lived only for the day. They were filled with a sense of hopelessness about the future. It has been said that hope is a precious element in the lives of all persons, but many aspects of the adolescent's situation make hope particularly essential.[3]

Few of the children I talked with participated in any of the clubs, hobbies, or sports that broaden the horizons of other adolescents. Few were involved in creative activities such as drama, painting, or playing a musical instrument. Few had strong interests in literature, theatre, dancing, or music. In relation to responsibility, some of the children already had so much that they had no desire for more. In fact, most said they wanted to escape it. Others had no challenge at all.

There is usually some defiance and hostility toward parents among adolescents; with the children in my study, these feelings were present much earlier. Most began to develop negative feelings toward parents soon after they became aware of problem drinking and parental disharmony. The average age at which they knew about these problems and reacted to them was six or seven; for a few, it was as early as four.

Particularly difficult for the adolescent is the experience of seeing his mother physically hurt or threatened.

> A child may be too small physically to interfere and yet mature enough to feel highly frustrated. He may be perplexed as to his duty and torn by internal conflict.... These are the children who are likely to become bitter, calculating, full of hatred for a parent or an entire family group.[4]

The implications of all this for the children I studied are great. They would seem to be facing life with more insecurity and less confidence in themselves and others than the average youngster. Few of them had any normal opportunity to test themselves in new tasks and experiences. While most children have times at which they feel uncertain of being wanted, understood, or loved, the children in my group seemed to be uncertain most of the time. Thus they are likely to have major problems in understanding themselves and in relating to or understanding others. Their attitudes toward life have been distorted because of the ideas they have acquired from their parents. An example is the attitude toward authority: if there is a lack of trust and an unwise use of authority by the parents, as was the case for many of the children in my study, a child is left with negative attitudes toward authority which he will carry over into adulthood; and resentment toward authority or inability to accept it is, according to one researcher,[5] one of the major characteristics of the adult alcoholic.

These children apparently had so many practical problems to contend with that they had little energy left to understand or to cope with their own emotional difficulties, and there was no one in their environment to help them. Only a few spoke of closeness to adults outside their family or of talking with them on a confidential basis. Most appeared to think that adults would not understand their problems. Because they felt no basic trust in their parents, they believed that adults generally could not be trusted. In any case, their reluctance to discuss their difficulties with adults outside the family was usually strengthened by the admonitions of the non-alcoholic parent.

This isolation takes on particular significance when we realize how vital it is for a child in a family devoid of strong positive relationships to have contact with other adults – such as an understanding teacher or an affectionate relative – who could provide some of the warmth he needs. Such an experience is vital in helping any child work through his problems. Without it, he is more likely to internalize them or to express them in anti-social behavior. He is also likely to develop feelings of hatred toward his parents and everyone else in his environment. He may even become convinced that the whole outside world is threatening and hostile. When we are seeking explanations for alienation among adolescents generally, it may be useful to remember that some of these young people have emerged from homes of the kind described in this study.

REFERENCES

1. FARNHAM, M. F. *The Adolescent.* New York: Harper and Bros., 1951.

2. COLE, L. *The Psychology of Adolescence.* New York: Rinehart, 1948.

3. JERSILD, A. T. *The Psychology of Adolescents.* New York: MacMillan, 1957.

4. BOSSARD, J. H. S. *The Sociology of Child Development.* New York, London: Harper and Bros., 1948.

5. LOLLI, G. On therapeutic success in alcoholism. *Pastoral Psychology.* 15: 41–47, 1964.

6. HORNEY, K. *The Neurotic Personality of our Times.* New York: W. W. Norton, 1937.

3.

The Parents

"I think if they really cared they could be different." So said Sara, a ten-year-old, as she talked to me about her parents. "They're always fighting; I feel like I'm in the middle of a great big storm. Once on my birthday Daddy threw my cake right in Mom's face because he was mad at her."

Fourteen-year-old Bryan said bitterly, "I never really feel that I know my parents. They act like a couple of kids – always quarrelling over every little thing. They just think of themselves. Sometimes I feel a hundred years older than them."

Lois, who is thirteen, commented: "Mom needs me to help her look after things, but I've never really thought she cared about me as a person. In our family we can't even talk decently to each other."

The comments of Charles, aged fifteen, were even more graphic. "You don't need parents – you can't talk sensibly to them. You learn to find the answers in books. I'm different than other kids. I have to put Mom to bed when she's drunk and keep the liquor from her – you can't say that's normal."

When I asked Roger, aged sixteen, about his home life he said, "A family is a few kids – boys and girls – a mother to love and look after you and a father who teaches and helps you. You do things together – you all like each other." Bitterly he added, "My family has never been like that."

In assessing all the children's interviews, I found there was not one child who had described his family life as normal or like that of most other families. Three children said it might be normal if there were no parental fighting or drinking, and two said it might be normal if there were no fighting. While a few children blamed the alcoholic parent alone for the family situation and an equal number blamed the non-alcoholic parent alone, most blamed both parents.

It was interesting to note that where several children came from the same family, all of them described their parents in much the same way. Either all the children blamed both parents for their poor family life or all blamed one particular parent.

Many of the children seemed desperately to want a family life like that of other children. Tragically, 23

said they were not really part of a family and that they
felt no positive bond with any other member of the
family. Most disturbing of all were 17 children who
seemed to have lost all sense of caring whether they
had a family. "Families are no good – they're useless.
You just have to depend on yourself."

While in most instances it was the children in the
older age group who appeared to be most estranged,
there were a few exceptions. In one family of three
children, two who were twelve and fourteen said they
had lost interest in family living whereas the middle
child, who was thirteen, said he still hoped for some
improvement.

It is probable that a great many families in our
society do not come anywhere near reaching any ideal
concept of a family life, but the average family does
provide in reasonable degree those conditions that
enable a child to grow into healthy adulthood. In comparing the families in my study with an expert's pro-
jected ideal family,[1] it would appear that on most
counts the alcoholic's family, as his children described
it, must fall very far below the achievement of the
average family – let alone the ideal. While in most
instances there appeared to be reasonably adequate
physical care of the children, their emotional needs
seemed to be almost entirely unmet. Apparently, there
was practically no sensitivity to these needs, and com-
munication was hostile and negative; overall security
and encouragement seemed quite absent, as did pro-
ductive relationships both inside and outside the family.
These parents seemed to be inhibiting the children's
growth as they fed on them to meet their own needs;
at the same time, they were also inhibiting their own

growth as parents.

Although not many of these families had been able to help themselves, only a few had sought outside help other than treatment for the alcoholic member. Family roles seemed ill-defined, grossly distorted, or non-existent. The many crises caused by drinking, loss of job, or separation were destructive, and there appeared to be little mutual respect between family members and little unity or cooperation.

In my sample of parents there were 53 alcoholic fathers and 19 alcoholic mothers. Such a proportion of male to female alcoholics is seldom reported in studies of alcoholism: there are generally thought to be about five times as many alcoholic men as women. My figures tend, instead, to support some more recent thinking which suggests that there is considerable hidden alcoholism among women and that the ratio of men to women is probably much lower. Of course, the method by which I involved these particular parents in my study might also have had something to do with this. (See pages 100–104.)

The parents in my study were between the ages of thirty-five and fifty, married for a good many years, with families of one to ten children. There was one common-law union of fairly long duration. In almost all instances the fathers were steadily employed and earned more than enough to support their families. Although many had changed jobs frequently, there was only one instance of long-term unemployment. A few had held the same position for over 10 years.

Long before I made an analysis of the parents in my study, I was curious about why certain parents, but not others, would permit their children to take part in a research project in which the children would be called upon to talk frankly about them to an outsider. A look at interview participation in relation to the father's education reveals that only about one third of fathers with elementary school or high school education accepted. Among those with a university education, a higher proportion – almost half – accepted. Similarly, an analysis of acceptance in relation to father's occupation shows that a considerably higher proportion of those in the upper occupational groups accepted.

A look at participation in relation to acceptance of treatment (as defined on page 105) reveals little. Slightly less than half of the parents who had had treatment agreed to have their children interviewed, and a slightly higher proportion of those who had had no treatment accepted. Few of those who had received treatment had achieved abstinence, and a slightly greater proportion of those who were still drinking agreed to have their children take part in the study.

Only by means of a more intensive study of the individual parents, which was beyond the scope of this project, could one hope to discover the answer to this motivational puzzle. Nevertheless, I had a strong feeling that an underlying desire to make a worthwhile contribution to the understanding of a major social problem might have played a part in determining the response of those parents who permitted their children to participate in the study.

*Father should be able to support us, but he doesn't.
I hate it when mother goes to work.*

For the most part, the father was the primary wage earner, though the mother was playing that role in seven cases of separation. In 31 instances where the couples were together, the mother indicated that she was working because the father's earnings were spent on drinking or on impulsive, inappropriate purchases in other areas. In a few cases, the mother said she was working mainly to escape the tensions of the home.

As I looked into the backgrounds of the children, I found that almost half of them had mothers who were working outside the home. Their overt reactions to their mothers' working varied widely, but almost every child expressed some negative feelings about it. More than 25 per cent said that they missed their mothers' presence at lunch time or after school, and about 50 per cent said they disliked having their mothers work and felt rejected because of it. Nearly all said they thought that their fathers should be able to support the family. Saddest of all were the children (about one third of those with employed mothers) who said that it did not matter to them whether their mothers worked or not because their mothers were not important to them. Many were quick to admit, however, that the added income was welcome in that it supplied money to pay debts and buy things they wanted and needed. Some of these children had an older brother or sister who attempted to take the working mother's place as homemaker.

For many of the children, their mothers' jobs seemed also to increase their hostility toward their father. The family seemed to suffer more when the mother took over part of the father's role and spent less time in homemaking. For most of these children, this was just one more way in which they felt different and isolated.

A child must discover for himself the experiences of trusting others....

To round out the picture of family life, it may be relevant to comment on the alcoholic's family and its relation to organized religion. Half the children in my study had no consistent contact with any church. Only a few families out of the total group attended as a family. In most of the churchgoing families, the alcoholic member had achieved more than a year of abstinence, and thus we might infer that there was some connection between abstinence and church attendance. However, when I reviewed these children's reactions to family life it seemed that their existence, too, was far from normal. In all but one instance, in fact, I had classified the children from these homes among the more seriously affected. In only rare instances did there seem to be a close bond between a priest, pastor, or a church-school teacher and any member of the recovered alcoholic's family. In families where the children attended church with the non-alcoholic parent and in families where the children attended on their own, the picture was much the same.

Many authorities believe that religious concepts are most effectively communicated when they are associated with daily life. "Learning materials presented in church or Sunday school are not enough. A child must discover for himself the experiences of trusting others, co-operating, and the nature of goodness and love."[2] The child in an alcoholic family has generally encountered few, if any, of these qualities in his family life. For many of them, therefore, attendance at a church or church school would seem to be meaningful more as an escape from home than as a means to spiritual growth.

Why did they have us at all if they weren't going to care about us?

Research suggests that the most important external influence for any child is the emotional relationship between the child and his parents. The greater the breakdown in affectionate relationships, the more the emotional development of the child will be distorted.[3] The interviews in this study present a vivid picture of emotional separation between parents and children. Only two children appeared to enjoy a close relationship with their alcoholic fathers and only four with their non-alcoholic mothers. A few felt close to one parent or the other at times when there was a respite from fighting and drinking, but most of the children said they felt generally rejected by both parents. They seem to feel the rejection of their non-alcoholic mother more keenly than that of their alcoholic father. It was as though they saw him as someone with a handicap and so believed that he could not help treating them as he did. They tended to make excuses for him that they did not make for the non-alcoholic parent.

She *could be different. She doesn't need to fight
with him or nag us, even if he* is *drinking.*

Much has been written about parents in general, but
little about alcoholics and their mates as fathers and
mothers. The importance of the father's role in any
family has been emphasized. In one study it is stated:
"The presence of a wise affectionate father gives to
the child a sense of security in life, a control upon which
he can rest and within which he can adventure, an ideal
toward which he can ... strive. Father is a protector and
is needed not only as someone to love but also as a
pattern and control in the child's development."[4]

One social worker, in a study of alcoholic fathers,
has noted a lack of easy, relaxed relationships between
the fathers and their children.[5] In her study, the
majority of fathers had more of a sibling than a parental
relationship with their children. She saw fathers vying
with their children for the mothers' affection and
attention.

In my own experience, alcoholic fathers appear to
be self-centered and unable to have close, satisfying
relationships with anyone – least of all with their wives
and children, particularly when the children are past
infancy. They seem to be poor models for their children
and quite unable to understand them, to love them in a
mature way, or to teach them.[6] It seems to make
matters worse that the father in his periods of sobriety
may seem "charming, affectionate, understanding, and
penitent."

From such episodes a child may gain an impression of
omnipotence and loving kindness. The disillusionment of
the drinking episode is shattering to the child. He is

frequently subjected to alternating experiences of exalted hopes and blighting disappointments which cause him to show a bewildering array of conflicting feelings, inconsistencies, and antagonisms.[7]

The non-alcoholic mother has been exhaustively described in the literature.[8] Her unmet needs are often as great as those of the alcoholic. Although she usually gives her children adequate physical care, she is frequently no better than the alcoholic at relating warmly or closely to them. As one expert has put it, the non-alcoholic mother is usually likely to lose some of her ability to relate closely to her children as she becomes more and more absorbed in her own frustration and anger. She tends, as did most of the mothers in my study, to lose sight of the needs and rights of children beyond such basics as shelter, food, and clothing. By contrast, she often becomes more mothering to her alcoholic husband than she is to her children.[9]

In instances in my study where the mother was the alcoholic, the children also described both parents as unable to have a strong, satisfying relationship with one another or their children. In addition, the children described the non-alcoholic father as too busy doing his own job and the mother's to pay very much attention to their needs.

The personal needs of the alcoholic and his spouse, to them, are overwhelming. They do not willfully neglect their children; but their constant quarrelling, their inability to recognize or meet their children's needs, and their failure to love wisely and to understand their children would seem to constitute a form of rejection that clearly amounts to neglect.

Such parents, according to a well known social scientist, seldom wish to hurt their children. It is merely that their self-interest seems to be so great at times that it obscures everything and everyone else. "The needs of the children intrude upon that self-interest as irritants. Children require physical care, guidance, control, attention, affection, and patience – all the qualities the parents are themselves, like children, demanding from one another and from a denying world."[10]

Frequently the separations were short and the reunions based upon economics or a blind hope that the alcoholic's promises to stop drinking would solve all of the couple's problems.

In viewing these unhappy marriage partners, it was only natural to wonder about the nature of the bond that had held so many of them together for so long. While few were legally separated, many were as good as separated in the eyes of the children. It was common for the husband to remain out of the home during and beyond his drinking periods. Many of the husbands and wives were not sleeping together or even eating meals together. They rarely shared any outside activities. When they did, the wife usually went along mainly as a watch-dog over her husband's drinking. The study revealed no instances of shared planning for the home or the children. In short, these marriages seemed to be held together not by bonds of mutual interest or by a sense of responsibility for the children but rather by extreme neurotic interaction.

One might also conjecture that many of these marriages were held together by apathy and fear – apathy resulting in a basic inability to take any definite action to change the situation, and fear resulting from unwillingness to lose the mutual satisfaction derived from overly emotional interdependence. Those who separated rarely did so on a planned, rational basis, but rather as an impulsive act engendered by overwhelming pressure or by a desire to punish the alcoholic or to prove that he was not important.

Since Dad got sober I've had the most peaceful time of my life, but things are not much better between us.

Fifteen of the alcoholic parents in this study had been abstinent for periods of one to five years. In five of these cases, both parents were alcoholic but only one of the marital partners had achieved abstinence. Because of the tremendous amount of effort directed at this outcome, it seems important to take a particular look at these families. What was the effect of abstinence on family life?

The answer, rather surprisingly, seems to be that the home situations of the children of these abstainers were not much different from those of the other children in the study. One boy of fifteen summed it up: "Dad's changed now that he's not drinking. He's friendlier, and he talks more. Sometimes he even tries to act like a father and makes some rules, but he still never sticks to what he says. I think he's afraid we won't love him if he does. My parents don't fight quite as much now, but they're not really happy. Mom never lets Dad forget about his drinking days. She's still the one who runs things. Dad seems more like one of us kids."

A girl of twelve commented: "Dad takes Mom to a

show occasionally now, but we still don't see much of him. He's always working overtime or at AA meetings. Sometimes we go places together or he helps me with my homework, but Mom and Dad still don't have much of a life together. We're not really like a family."

A boy of fourteen complained that although his father was no longer drinking, he was still hard to talk to. "My parents are really not interested in us. I'll never forget those years, and I always wonder whether he will start drinking again."

"There's still a lot of tension between Mom and Dad," said a thirteen-year-old. "It makes me feel scared of people, especially men. Even though Dad doesn't drink now, I don't like what I've seen of marriage. Mom and Dad are always pretending to other people that everything's fine now, but I think they're like a couple of ostriches, hiding their heads in the sand."

Only four children, all in one family, said they felt that things were "really good now that Dad's sober." In this family, the father – in contrast to nearly all other fathers in the study – was still in treatment. It was evident that a number of factors had influenced the recovery in their family life. First, the children were all relatively young. Second, the family relationships during the drinking years had not been as severely distorted – particularly the relationship between the mother and the children. Third, the mother had been able to take definite action, such as leaving the father and refusing to return until he had been sober for six months. Even in this family, however, three of the children were still fearful. "I still want to be sure Dad's really OK before I get to know anyone too well," said one. "I'm not sure yet in my mind. We're all so happy, it's sort of scary now. I don't understand how Mom and Dad could have changed so much, and that's why I'm still worried. I sure hope things stay this way."

It is not difficult to see that even though abstinence improves the lot of certain children in some respects, the situation in the homes of recovered alcoholics may still be far from normal. Often, relationships between the parents still seem strained, and those between parents and children far from positive. The behavior and attitudes of the father and mother have not changed essentially, and the children are still being affected.

Much of the alcoholic's behavior is caused by ... steady withdrawal of respect and affection.

While I have tended throughout to emphasize the effect of poor parental relationships on the children, it is important also to recognize that the attitudes of the children are in turn felt and reacted to by the parents. "Relationships between the alcoholic and his family are not one-way. [He has a] sense of isolation from other family members and [of] their steady withdrawal of respect and affection."[11] The same might be said of the non-alcoholic parent. Thus both parents are probably reacting constantly to the rejection of themselves by their children, and this would only serve to increase their negative behavior and sense of failure as parents.

I still wouldn't want any other parents.

From all that has been presented it seems evident that most of the parents of the children in this study are perceived by their children as deeply unhappy, insecure and torn by many emotional needs. The intensity of the parents' obsessive involvement with one another *and* the presence of alcoholism has led to considerable rejection and virtual neglect of their children. Nevertheless, it should be emphasized that most of the children expressed a basic liking for their parents. Many said they would not want any other parents; they only wanted a chance to know and to be understood by the parents they had.

REFERENCES

1. OTTO, H. What is a strong family? *Journal of Marriage and Family Living.* 24: 77–80, 1962.

2. BRECKENRIDGE, M. E. and VINCENT, E. L. *Child Development.* Philadelphia: W. I. B. Saunders, 1960.

3. SAUL, L. J. and WENAR, S. Early influences on disorders of personality. *Psychoanalytical Quarterly.* 34: 327–389, 1965.

4. ISAACS, S. *Fatherless Children.* London: Routledge and Kegan Paul, 1948.

5. JACKSON, M. J. A follow up study of the relationship between drinking behaviour and participation in child care activities. Master's thesis, School of Social Work, University of Toronto, 1958.

6. CORK, R. M. Alcoholism and the family. Paper presented at the Alcoholism and Drug Addiction Research Foundation Summer Course; reprinted by Education Division of the Foundation, Toronto, 1964.

7. NEWELL, N. Alcoholism and the father image. *Quarterly Journal of Studies on Alcohol.* 11: 92–96, 1950.

8. PRICE, G.M . A study of the wives of twenty alcoholics. *Journal of Psychiatric Social Work*. 23 (1): 37–41, 1953.

   FUTTERMAN, S. Personality trends in wives of alcoholics. *Journal of Psychiatric Social Work*. 23 (1): 37–41, 1953.

   WHALEN, T. Wives of alcoholics; four types observed in a family service agency. *Quarterly Journal of Studies on Alcohol*. 14: 632–641, 1953.

   KOGAN, K. L. and JACKSON, J. K. Stress, personality and emotional disturbance in wives of alcoholics. *Quarterly Journal of Studies on Alcohol*. 26: 486–495, 1965.

9. FOX, R. The alcoholic spouse. In: Eisenstein, V .W., ed., *Neurotic Interaction in Marriage*. New York: Basic Books, 1952.

10. YOUNG, L. *Wednesday's Children*. New York: McGraw-Hill, 1964.

11. JACKSON, J. K. Alcoholism and the family. *Annals of the American Academy of Political and Social Sciences*. 315: 90–98, 1958.

4.

What has happened to these Children?

"I always feel sad and worried – mostly just awful mad at them for the way they are," said Judy, a ten-year-old, as she tried to tell me how she had been affected. "There's just always screaming in our house – it makes me get all funny inside – frightened like. The little ones get mad at me because they have to mind me when Mom can't manage them. Mommy always screams at me because I keep forgetting to do all the things she tells me to do, and I can't keep the little kids quiet enough when she has a headache. I can't talk to Daddy or Mommy about how I feel – they just get madder. I always dream it will be better – but I know it never will.

"I keep wishing my parents were like other parents," said Judy. "They're so unhappy. I keep worrying about what will happen to me if Mom gets sick – she just has this one lung – and Daddy keeps having to go to jail. I feel so awful I keep thinking of dying."

Nora, who is thirteen, told me: "It's the awful things they say to each other and the fighting that makes me upset. I can't do my homework very well when they're fighting. They never agree on anything – we just all do what we like when we want to. Dad tells us we can do things because Mom says we can't. He buys us things we don't need and never gets us the things we do need. I'm always confused – I never know who to listen to even when he isn't drinking. Sometimes he hits us or Mom. I feel too grown up, I worry all the time – I haven't any friends. I guess I wouldn't even mind about the drinking if they'd be happier – no one is happy. Take me, I'm too fat. I always eat too much when I'm unhappy and that's most of the time, but no one seems to care. Once I got so depressed I tried to commit suicide. I can't talk to anyone because no one would understand. I know I'll have to get away as soon as I can. A family is no good to you."

Sixteen-year-old Scott had a mother who was an alcoholic. "I used to sneak her the beer after my Dad had hidden it, because it made her nicer. I didn't mind the drinking then – now I'm ashamed of her – disgusted. Mom is different when she is drinking – not rational – sort of sentimental and less organized. We never get any regular meals. You can't talk to her. She never minds what you do or where you are, so long as you are on her side. The teachers tell me I've got a good brain. But I can't use it; I've given up on school.

"I've never been really close to Dad," Scott continued. "He's not a person you can know easily – you have to do everything he wants – nothing pleases him – he's always at Mom for her poor housekeeping. All the fighting makes me more high-strung – more emotional. They never think of us. It's impossible not to take sides. Sometimes you're on one side and then on the other. Each one indoctrinates you with propaganda against the other. I've never really felt close to either of them. I've learned not to expect anything from them – or anyone. I just want to be left alone. They are both just a couple of selfish people who shouldn't have kids. I know I'll never get married – it's stupid – you're tied to a woman who drinks and she just doesn't take her responsibilities to her children."

These excerpts from interviews with three children were fairly typical. Their words strongly indicate that they have been affected in their school work and in their relationships both in and out of the home. They seem confused and upset by their parents' behavior and worried about their position with their peers. Their needs are neither recognized nor met by either parent, and their feelings seem to be completely overlooked. Some seem to suffer physically, and nearly all appear to suffer emotionally.

These children easily become upset, angry, and defiant. Above all, they feel parental rejection. Some accept the situation passively, while others become hostile and seek escape. They are overly concerned with the future to the point of worrying about their own marriages because they are uncertain about the opposite sex or because they think family life is not worthwhile. Table II gives an overall picture of the various ways all the children felt they had been affected.

TABLE II

THE CHILDREN'S VIEW: HOW THEY WERE AFFECTED

Effect	No. of Children Affected
A. Not affected	0
School work affected	54
Relationships within family affected	113
Relationships outside of family affected	111
Physical health suffered	10
B. Worries constantly about not being liked by peers	46
Worries constantly about being different	73
Is generally anxious and afraid of future	70
Feels burdened by too much responsibility – has had to grow up too fast	48
Is constantly ashamed, feels hurt, gets upset, and cries readily	89
Is never sure of self, lacks self-confidence	108
C. Feels unwanted by one or both parents	112
Is constantly angry, hostile toward parents and others	75
Is overly self-reliant, feels unable to trust or depend on anyone	31
Feels uncomfortable with or fearful of the opposite sex	48
Is constantly defiant, at odds with authority	54
Feels hopeless and depressed, lacks ambition, but passively accepts situation	25
Thinks constantly of escaping from family or from responsibilities generally	50

Section A of the table shows the most tangible effects. While only a small percentage of the children spoke of definite physical effects, these were fairly serious. They included one case of bed-wetting at fifteen; two of unspecified nervous conditions of lengthy duration; one three-year history of ulcers; three cases of obesity; one history that encompassed jaundice, pneumonia, and chronic asthma; and several cases of chronic stomach-ache.

Sections B and C show the ways in which the children felt they had been damaged emotionally. While this might well be a picture of children in troubled homes generally, it seems probable that the presence of constant excessive drinking provided considerable additional stress and strain.

It was not possible in a study such as this to make any precise assessment of the degree of damage to any one child. Nonetheless, through repeated readings of each interview and weighing of the child's qualitative responses concerning certain vital areas of his life experience, I was able to group the children in terms of the amount of damage they appeared to have suffered. Details of the organization of the data may be found in the Appendix, and the results of my assessment are shown below.

TABLE III

INTERVIEWER'S ASSESSMENT OF DAMAGE TO THE CHILDREN

Amount of Damage	No. of Children
None	0
Slight	9
Fairly serious	56
Very serious	50

The term *slight* was applied to those children who said they still had some positive identification with one parent even though they were unable to confide in this parent. They tended to resent the parental drinking and fighting, but in between such episodes they were not as upset and felt hopeful that things would eventually change for the better. These children were, like most of the others, worried and anxious. To some extent their school work had been affected as well as their relationships in and out of the home. In other ways they did not seem to be deeply harmed. Since this group included proportionately more of the younger children, I wondered whether it was just a matter of time until they would be more seriously affected.

The children who were classified as being damaged in a *fairly serious* way included those who said they were more or less constantly at odds with, and felt rejected by, one or both parents. They still, however, seemed to have a positive tie with the family in spite of a sense of hopelessness – a feeling that things would never be different. While they appeared to suffer in the ways indicated by items in sections A and B (Table II), they did not seem so severely damaged that they could not have responded readily if counselling had been available.

Those who were classified as *very seriously* affected seemed to have suffered in many ways similar to the other two groups of children. In addition, they appeared to have been damaged in ways indicated by section C. These children had the most destructive type of relationship with their parents; it showed up as

constant resentment or open hatred. They seemed to
feel that the family had little or no value and were
emotionally isolated from all other family members.
These children, in my opinion, would need intensive
and long-term therapy if these problems were not to
be permanent.

One well-known writer on alcoholism has said that
"adverse circumstances, illness or accidents may affect
any individual in his daily routine or in his family life
in several ways at once, for a period of a week, a month
or a year, but rarely do they affect all his life activities
and affect them all adversely. Alcoholism does. When
it strikes it hits the alcoholic's entire existence."[1] Much
the same sort of comparison might be made between
the children in any other type of troubled home and
the children of alcoholics. For most of them, their
entire existence seems to be threatened at many levels.

In reviewing the interviews, it became clear that the
children felt more deeply affected by *disharmony and
rejection* than by excessive drinking. This does not
mean that they were not concerned about their parents'
drinking or that it did not play a significant part in
creating their problems. It does mean, however, that
for most of them it was perceived as a secondary cause
of their difficulties and as much less hard to take than
the constant parental unhappiness and quarrelling.
The table that follows summarizes the children's comments on what bothered them most about their family
situation. Since each child responded in several ways,
the total number of children is not significant. (This
holds true for most of the tables presented in the re-
mainder of this chapter.)

TABLE IV

THE CHILDREN'S FOCUS OF CONCERN IN THEIR FAMILY LIFE

Focus of Concern	No. of Children Concerned
Drinking	1
Drunkenness	6
Parental fighting and quarrelling	98
Unhappiness of parent	35
Lack of interest of alcoholic parent	96
Lack of interest of non-alcoholic parent	73

Traditionally the alcoholic has generally had to bear full blame for the disruption in his family life, and most attempts to help the family have been concentrated on treatment of the drinking problem. The results shown above are particularly interesting when viewed in this light.

It is significant that a large number of children said that they were rejected by *both parents*, the non-alcoholic one as well as the alcoholic. It is also interesting to note that the children's attitudes to drinking covered a wide spectrum.

Clearly there is much resentment among the children about the consequences of drinking. Many expressed intense feelings of shame concerning an alcoholic parent, and many said they were ashamed of both parents. While more than half the children said they were not concerned about drinking if it did not lead to drunkenness or fighting, nearly a third indicated resentment concerning the amount of attention their mothers devoted to their alcoholic fathers.

TABLE V

THE CHILDREN'S REACTION TO DRINKING

Reaction	*No. of Children Reacting*
OK to drink	1
OK to drink but not to get drunk or fight	67
OK to drink if non-alcoholic parent wouldn't get upset	12
Understands why parent has to drink, feels sorry for him	14
Frightened of parent when drinking	19
Ashamed, embarrassed, disgusted by drinking	81
Angry, resentful, hurt by consequences of drinking	76
Resentful of family focus on alcoholic or the drinking	37
Against drinking by fathers or mothers	26
Against any drinking	19

Only a few of the children were opposed to drinking by adults generally, and only a few were against any drinking by their parents. Interestingly, more children were against their mothers' drinking than their fathers'. (This seems to reflect the double standard of society which says women should not drink to excess.) They seemed to feel that a woman shouldn't drink, and described maternal drinking as "not nice – not like a mother." More practical reasons were advanced against paternal drinking: "He spends all our money on drink." "He loses jobs." "He goes to jail."

Non-alcoholic parents are believed by their children to have markedly different attitudes, however. As the following table shows, most of the non-alcoholic parents were seen as being strongly against drinking.

TABLE VI

THE CHILDREN'S VIEW OF THE NON-ALCOHOLIC PARENT'S REACTION TO DRINKING

View of Parent's Reaction	No. of Children
OK to drink	3
OK to drink but not to get drunk or fight	23
Fears drinking may cause accidents or fire	5
Angry, hurt by consequences	13
Against drinking by women	6
Against drinking by men	14
Against any drinking, hates it	51
	115

One partner's strongly negative attitude toward the excessive drinking of the other must, of course, be a source of considerable conflict within a marriage. Where a mother's dislike of drinking is more intense than that of her children, this may also provide a source of some conflict.

Most of the children were, of course, aware that some of the problems in their families were caused by drinking, and Table VII shows the kinds of problems they felt it caused and how many children were concerned about each problem.

TABLE VII

THE CHILDREN'S VIEWS OF THE PROBLEMS CAUSED BY EXCESSIVE DRINKING

Problems	No. of Children Concerned
No particular problems	0
Money problems	72
Non-alcoholic parent unduly upset	87
Parents are inconsistent, unpredictable	108
People don't like you, pity you, you feel different	82
Physical abuse between parents, destructive behavior on part of the alcoholic	28
Accidents to alcoholic parent, or jail	18
Loss of respect for alcoholic parent, ashamed of him	81
Destroys alcoholic parent or the family	14

It is obvious from this that most children felt that their major problem was the inconsistency or unpredictability of *both* parents, not just of the alcoholic. A large number of children were also greatly disturbed by the effect of the alcoholic parent on the non-alcoholic one. "She's always worried. She's terribly tense from fighting with him all the time." For the most part, however, their reaction did *not* appear to be concern for the suffering of the non-alcoholic parent. It was rejection of that parent's behavior to her children, coupled with the belief that her behavior was caused indirectly by her dealings with the alcoholic. An almost equal number of children saw the problem as one that directly affected them. "The way my parents are makes me feel different. I'm always afraid no one will like me. Some people pity me. Others probably think I'm the same type as my parents."

Loss of respect for the alcoholic parent appeared great as a problem for a number of the children, but in most instances there was *also* a loss of respect for the non-alcoholic parent. "I'm too ashamed to let my friends know how they are. How can you respect them when they act like they do?" Under such circumstances, the growth of a child's self-image and self-confidence must proceed with great difficulty.

In spite of the fact that the joint income of most of the fathers and mothers was more than adequate, a large proportion of the children were keenly aware of debts and other financial problems attributable to drinking. "Dad makes good money, but there's never enough. Some weeks we have hamburger every day. He buys things we don't need when my little brother needs shoes. We always have debts, and Mom makes me lie to the bill-collectors when they come to the door. You never have the money to do the things other kids do."

More than a quarter of the children talked about experiences with physical violence, destructiveness, accident-proneness, or jailing. These were obviously searing experiences – very often the earliest and perhaps the most lasting memories of trouble in their homes.

"I'll always remember the way he broke all Mom's best things. He's spoiled every Christmas I can remember because he smashes the tree."

"I always worried that he'd die when he kept falling down."

"None of the other kids I know have fathers who go to jail. I never want to go out of the house."

In an attempt to understand their concept of the alcoholic or alcoholism, I asked each child to tell me what these words meant to them. A few children, particularly the older ones, said that alcohol destroyed the alcoholic. "His mind isn't right. He acts like he's a crazy person." "She's so destroyed, she'll never be the same even though she's sober." About an equal number of children said that alcoholism permanently destroyed family life. All of them, even the youngest, attempted a definition.

TABLE VIII

THE CHILDREN'S DEFINITION OF AN ALCOHOLIC OR OF ALCOHOLISM

Definition	No. of Children
1. A person who drinks too much, drinks constantly	27
2. A person who has to drink to escape, can't do anything else	58
3. A person who is stupid, selfish, not grown up, hurts other people	16
4. A person who is worried, unhappy, sick, afraid of life	29
5. Something that's a waste of money	2
6. Something that's a bad habit	7
7. Something that makes you a different person	1
8. Something that destroys or ruins a person	5

It is interesting to note how many of the children describe alcoholism in *internal* rather than external terms – as something that is happening within a person rather than as some outer force acting on him. It is evident from this table that most of the children felt that an alcoholic was a person who could not help constantly making excessive use of alcohol – as a person who *had* to drink. Many children saw him as a person whose need to drink was stronger than his will to do anything else – for example, his desire to meet the needs of his family.

If we take items 3 and 4 together, however, we can see that nearly as many children gave a definition in which they described the *kind of person* they thought the alcoholic was. Obviously, these children have made some effort to understand the reasons for their parents' drinking. In spite of the fact that money problems (as shown in Table VII) loomed large in many of their homes, most of the children did not define alcoholism as a waste of money.

Another question posed to each child was that of his attitude to drinking in relation to his own future. Again, even the youngest had already formed an opinion.

Most of the children said they would not drink, with the major reasons being fear of becoming like the alcoholic parent, belief that drinking disrupts family life, belief that drinking is wrong on health or moral grounds or "because it hurts other people." The awareness that drinking can hurt other people is very significant when we consider that, according to the literature, the lives of at least four or five other persons, on the average, are damaged by each alcoholic.

TABLE IX
THE CHILDREN'S ATTITUDE TO THEIR OWN FUTURE
USE OF ALCOHOL

Attitude	*No. of Children*
May drink at parties or special occasions	12
May drink but not like alcoholic parent does	25
Won't drink, stupid, disgusting, don't like taste of it	10
Won't drink, waste of money	4
Won't drink, afraid of getting like parent	32
Won't drink, upsets family life	15
Won't drink, not healthy, wrong to drink, hurts other people	15
Won't drink, women shouldn't drink	2
Won't drink, no one should drink	6
Drinking now	5

A few children were already drinking and had experienced intoxication. A good many more had tasted alcoholic beverages – usually as a result of being encouraged by the alcoholic parent to taste the dregs of his drink. If we take into account the children who are already drinking in some regular way, as well as those who said that they intended to drink as adults, we find that well over a third are interested in drinking. These particular children gave me special cause for concern because it happens that they were also among the most disturbed members of the group. Unless they get outside help, they would appear to be among those most likely to misuse alcohol or become dependent on it as adults.

It seemed important to take a particular look at the five children who were drinking in a regular way. One investigator has described the adolescent problem drinker as "one to whom drinking has become a problem of major significance in that there is repeated imbibing of alcoholic beverages which is in opposition to social pressure and which interferes with his education or employment." Children classified in this way reported "excessive drinking several times a week, involving a wide variety of beverages as well as hangovers, shakiness and blackouts."[2]

While the five children in my study had not quite reached this point, two said they had experienced passing out, three expressed strong liking for the feeling alcohol gave them and said that their school work was being seriously affected, and all were drinking in defiance of parental wishes.

In conclusion, it seems strikingly evident that all the children were affected traumatically to some degree by virtue of being the children of alcoholic parents. While most of the children were very keenly aware of the meaning of alcoholism, a significant number were prepared to drink as adults (somewhat blindly hoping they would not drink to the extent their parents did), and a few were drinking already to an unusual extent for their age. This does not necessarily mean that these few children are more likely to become alcoholics than any other children in the study. The fact that there seemed to be underlying personality disturbances in *all* the children does, however, suggest that should any of them turn to alcohol to meet some of their emotional needs, there is a very real possibility that they will become alcoholics.

REFERENCES

1. BACON, S. The mobilization of community resources. *Quarterly Journal of Studies on Alcohol.* 8: 473–497, 1947.

2. MACKAY, J .R. Clinical observation on adolescent problem drinkers. *Quarterly Journal of Studies on Alcohol.* 22: 124–134, 1961.

5.
Yesterday's Forgotten Children?

"I always wonder what makes them act like they do. What makes them so mean and unhappy? Why did they ever have children if they didn't want to be parents?" These questions and similar ones were frequently asked by children in my study. As I reread their interviews, I began more and more to share their curiosity. It seemed unlikely that their parents had willfully set out to harm them. In fact, it seemed much more probable that these adults, like most others, had had a real desire to be better fathers and mothers than their own parents had been.

While my study was focussed on the children and not on their parents, I had gained from the parents' clinic files* and from my conversations with them a certain amount of data about their own parents and about their family backgrounds. Was it possible that this might offer some clues to what lay behind their negative marital relationships and their behavior toward their children? I began to speculate about the relation of their backgrounds to their alcoholism and to wonder about the likelihood of alcoholism occurring in the third and fourth generations of these families.

As I assembled my data, it soon became evident that a large proportion of the alcoholics in my study had themselves had parents who, in their own words, "were not compatible" or "quarrelled frequently and excessively." While a few tended to idealize their parents, most said they had felt no close relationships between themselves and their mothers, between themselves and their fathers, or between themselves and both parents. Frequent references were made to stern, dominating fathers and to fathers who were often away from home. Several alcoholics vividly recalled physical abuse of themselves or of their mothers. A large number mentioned lack of financial support on the part of their fathers. Others expressed the view that they had had to shoulder undue responsibility at an early age in bringing up younger brothers and sisters or in helping to meet the family's financial needs. They frequently referred to their mothers as tense, worried, hard-working women who had little time for them individually,

---

*See Appendix.

or as women who were overly absorbed in their husbands and their husbands' drinking problems. A number reported being placed in foster homes or with relatives when young.

From what the parents said, it seemed evident that a high proportion of the alcoholic parents had had a deprived or distorted family background. Almost a third had experienced in early childhood the loss of a parent by separation or death. They claimed that they had rarely found a satisfying replacement, frequently going from relative to relative, foster home to foster home. Research indicates that there is a direct relationship between parental loss in childhood and the development of alcoholism.[1]

In a well-known study on the background of alcoholics, it was found that a large percentage came from homes that were broken before adolescence. Serious maladjustments, including alcoholism and mental illness, were found in a high proportion of their fathers. There was evidence of rejection, cruelty, over-indulgence, and encouragement of dependence.[2]

Alcoholism was very common in the parents of the alcoholics in my study. Two thirds of their fathers and about 10 per cent of their mothers were referred to as alcoholics, and in about 15 per cent of cases there appeared to have been alcoholism in both parents. (In another study involving over 4,000 alcoholics, 52 per cent had alcoholic fathers or mothers.)[3]

Four alcoholics in my study described both their parents as total abstainers. In these homes, there was probably strong pressure on the children not to drink. This will often produce another generation of abstainers; in these families, however, pressure to abstain seems to have had the opposite effect. (Other factors would obviously enter in as well.)

It was interesting to note that six alcoholics described one of their parents as a total abstainer and the other as an alcoholic. This would provide a source of deep parental conflict – one of the other factors generally thought to predispose a person to alcoholism.[1] It has been suggested that this particular conflict gives alcohol a magic or forbidden quality that prevents the establishment of control over its use.

In the background of the non-alcoholic parent there was also a considerable amount of alcoholism. Among parents of the non-alcoholic spouse, over half of the fathers and about 7 per cent of the mothers were described as alcoholics. Two-thirds of the non-alcoholic parents said they had had poor relationships with their own parents during childhood, and almost a third had experienced loss of a parent through death or separation at an early age. Researchers theorize that loss of a mother at an early age has a profound effect on subsequent security. Loss of the mother means that the home is less likely to be kept intact than where there is loss of the father. However, where it is the father who is absent there is an increased likelihood of the remaining parent becoming dependent upon the children, and this can inhibit the children's natural growth toward independence.[1]

It seems evident, in short, that the family background of the non-alcoholic spouses in my study was generally as poor as that of the alcoholics. The non-alcoholics, too, spoke frequently of intense parental unhappiness, frequent quarrelling, and parental rejection. While the alcoholics reported negative relationships with both parents, most of their spouses spoke primarily of negative relationships with their fathers and of overidentification with their mothers. One might wonder whether this was a factor in their selection of alcoholics or potential alcoholics as husbands. In any event, we might hypothesize that the background of both the alcoholic and the non-alcoholic parent left them ill-prepared to make a satisfying marriage or to be wise parents unless they receive some outside help.

Among those who have studied the problem of causation in relation to alcoholism, it now seems widely accepted that alcoholism has no one single cause. Rather, it seems to be the result of an interplay of numerous factors. Many theories contain some speculation about the part played by family background, however, and it has been suggested that "the key to alcoholism lies in the inter-personal relationships within the family." Excessive conflict within the family produces persons with a high degree of inner tension, and such people may use alcohol to reduce anxiety.[4] Parental rejection or loss of parent through death or separation can create strong anxiety and hostility in a growing child by causing persistent frustration of basic needs. Here, too, alcohol may appear to offer a way out.[5]

One researcher[2] has pointed out that alcoholism in the great majority of cases is not so much the result of immediate stress as of earlier predisposition underlying some environmental stress. I have come to believe that the chief environmental stress for many of the parents in my study, as well as for *their* parents, was marriage and family life. From 15 years of counselling the alcoholic and his family, it has become evident to me that the drinking of countless men and women became a serious problem only after marriage, the arrival of children, or the end of the children's infancy.

Another researcher has pointed out that excessive drinking and a sound marital relationship are incompatible. Abuse of alcohol will wreck the economic and prestige structure of the family and cause performance in the normal roles of husband and wife to deteriorate. Excessive drinking also causes a breakdown in attitudes and activities that encourage close personal relationships. It allows selfishness, carelessness, and aggression. For the all-purpose intimate association that is the family, excessive use of alcohol is usually catastrophic.[6]

This brief picture of the parents' own family background strongly resembles the picture presented by the children I interviewed. It is a background of alcoholism, financial difficulty, premature assumption of adult responsibilities, parental rejection, and parental incompatibility.

Many of these parents, when they were children, must also have been fearful, frustrated, and in conflict. They, too, must have felt isolated from the support of friends of their own age and that of understanding parents or other adults from whom they might have received help with their problems. It would therefore appear that many of the parents of today's forgotten children were the forgotten children of their own generation. Very likely this played a part in their becoming alcoholics and making unhappy marriages, as a consequence of which they have become unable to provide a vital family life for their own children.

While both my data and the present-day theoretical understanding are limited, what we do know about these people and about alcoholism suggests strongly that alcoholism – like other negative aspects of family life – may well be passed on from generation to generation unless there is some kind of intervention.

REFERENCES

1. HILGARD, J. R. and NEWMAN, M. F. Early parental deprivation as a functional factor in the etiology of schizophrenia and alcoholism. *American Journal of Orthopsychiatry*. 33: 409–420, 1963.

2. MOORE, R. A. and RAMSEUR, F. A study of the background of 100 hospitalized veterans with alcoholism. *Quarterly Journal of Studies on Alcohol*. 21: 51–67, 1960.

3. JELLINEK, E. M. Heredity of the alcoholic. In: *Alcohol, Science and Society*. New Haven, Conn.: Quarterly Journal of Studies on Alcohol, 1945.

4. McCORD, W. and McCORD, J. with GUDEMEN, J. *Origins of Alcoholism*. Palo Alto, Calif.: Stanford University Press, 1960.

5. WAHL, C. W. Some antecedent factors in the family history of 100 alcoholics. *Quarterly Journal of Studies on Alcohol*. 17: 643–654, 1956.

6. BACON, S. D. Excessive drinking and the institution of the family. In: *Alcohol, Science and Society*. New Haven, Conn.: Quarterly Journal of Studies on Alcohol, 1945.

6.

Tomorrow's Adults and their Children

Only in recent years has there been any real attempt to help the alcoholic as a member of a family group. Because of the deeply disturbed nature of the relationship between the alcoholic and his spouse, professionals have found it difficult to involve both partners in marital counselling or family therapy. Therefore, in spite of the fact that therapists are more and more aware of the needs in this area, the major focus has remained on treatment of the alcoholic as an individual rather than on recovery of his whole family.

A notable exception to this is the work of Alanon and Alateen, which for many years have been attempting to modify and limit the impact of alcoholism on

family members. Alanon is an outgrowth of the AA*
program. Its purpose is to help the whole family to live
more effectively with the alcoholic. The Alanon groups
are chiefly comprised of non-alcoholic men and women
whose wives or husbands have a drinking problem.
Through group interaction and support, they try to increase their understanding of themselves and of the
role they may have been playing in the on-going drinking as well as in the disruption of family life.

Alateen is also a form of group therapy based on
the AA philosophy. It is available to any adolescent
who has an alcoholic parent. Identification with other
children who have similar problems and sharing experiences with them may give a child a better understanding of his parents' problems and, even more
importantly, a better self-image and increased self-
confidence.

Unfortunately, there are all too few Alanon and
Alateen groups. At the same time, many alcoholic and
non-alcoholic parents and their children cannot fit into
or accept either the AA philosophy or this kind of
group experience. For these individuals there *must* be
some other source of help such as individual professional counselling, joint marital counselling, or family
group therapy.

The results of the present study form the basis for a
number of recommendations concerning the treatment
of these alcoholics and their families. These recommendations also reflect my experience over many years

*Alcoholics Anonymous, a fellowship of men and women whose
purpose is to help themselves and one another to overcome
alcoholism.

and the views of many other professionals in the field in many parts of the world. There is nothing really new about these concepts, but I believe that it is important to re-emphasize them here.

The first recommendation is that we face the tremendous need for recognition and treatment of those families that have an alcoholic member before he and all the other members of his family are severely damaged.

Many factors make early case-finding difficult. One is the alcoholic's resistance to admitting the problem. Another is the non-alcoholic spouse's reluctance to seek help; sometimes as many as seven years may elapse before she will do so. Others are the family's ability to hide behind a facade of adequacy and the fact that many children of alcoholics conceal their problems rather than acting them out in ways that might attract the attention of educational, law enforcement, or other agencies.

In addition to earlier case-finding, there must be a change in our methods of treating the alcoholic's family. We have all too often assumed that once the drinking problem was under control all the other problems in the family would resolve themselves; but in the families in my study where the alcoholic had become abstinent, there seldom appeared to be much gain in family unity. Thus, attainment of total abstinence can no longer be accepted as the point at which treatment should stop. Rather, it should be viewed as a crucial point in the on-going treatment of the family and its individual members.

While treatment of the family may be provided by a wide variety of therapists, I believe that the social worker has a particularly vital role to play which has not yet been fully recognized or accepted. Besides giving direct treatment to the whole family, social workers can co-ordinate and supplement the efforts of other workers such as the physician, the psychiatrist, and the psychologist, who have their own specialized roles to play at various stages of recovery.

Family service agencies have always treated a few families in which alcoholism has been a major problem. In many instances, their efforts have been successful. Frequently, however, the alcoholic and the family are rejected as "untreatable" once it is clear that excessive drinking is a persistent problem. There has been the attitude that alcoholism must be treated by an "expert." The alcoholic is quickly referred to AA, to a psychiatrist, or to an alcoholism treatment centre. Family problems as such are often more or less neglected.

Inherent in social work practice is the hope and intention that a family may, through counselling, be able to move toward a more meaningful life together. Much as a mother with her first baby needs to learn how to look after it, so the alcoholic and his wife often need to learn about simple, effective methods of child rearing. They need to learn about roles in family life, about discipline, about give and take among family members, about understanding their children, and even about enjoying their children.

I believe that the social worker is particularly well fitted to assume the role of a good and wise parent to these very dependent, insecure people. In so doing, the worker must demonstrate affection and, at the same time, be able to set and maintain limits. He or she should be consistently patient and yet able to show feelings of anger, disappointment, or frustration when appropriate. He should have unlimited tolerance for failures, be able to give support to every effort, and at the same time provide guidance, protection, and discipline. Like an ideal parent, he should be able gradually to decrease the element of dependence in the relationship.

Obviously all these qualities are not found only in social workers, but I believe that social workers are particularly well qualified by attitude and training to meet the social and emotional needs of a large proportion of our alcoholic families. I also believe that if a concerted effort were made to reach out to these particularly troubled families at an early stage of alcoholism and to involve them in family therapy we would not have as many broken homes or as many "forgotten children."

The second recommendation emerging from this study concerns the need for more intensive treatment of the non-alcoholic spouse.**

Treatment of the non-alcoholic parent is not a matter of involving her as an adjunct to treatment of her alcoholic husband, but rather one of helping her with her own conflicts, emotional upsets, and inter-

---

**While the non-alcoholic spouse is usually the mother, everything that follows applies equally to the non-alcoholic father, although he rarely seeks help for the family.

personal difficulties within the family. The wife must be helped to understand and to accept responsibility for the part she may be playing in the continued drinking as well as in the disruption of family life and the lives of the children. Therapists as well as the family must come to see that with the changed environment that might result from changes in the non-alcoholic parent, the alcoholic may be more able to benefit from treatment.

The non-alcoholic wife usually seeks help only when things have reached a breaking point. Most frequently she asks simply that someone "do something" about her husband's drinking. She is usually very defensive about looking at her own behavior and conflicts and at how these are affecting the family. She may have a profound belief that she is a failure as a wife and mother; she may even believe that she is the sole cause of her husband's drinking problem. Without appropriate help, however, she is unable to express these fears. Often she has tried for a considerable period to "cure" her husband through nagging and threatening or indulging and over-protecting him, in the belief that these are the only ways to solve a problem that she so often sees only as profuse, willful drinking.

There is a good reason for believing that the social worker in his initial contact with the wife of an alcoholic should identify quickly with the suffering, anxiety, and desire to be a good mother that usually underlie her request for help. In such a warm, supportive relationship, she may become more able to examine some of her conflicting feelings and fears and be helped to make some modifications in her marital relationship and in her relationships with her children. It is of interest to note that out of the 52 non-alcoholic partners in my study, only eight had had any professional help or had attended Alanon.

The third recommendation is that there should be a new approach on the part of all treatment personnel to the alcoholic who is a family man.

There has been too little attention to aspects of his condition other than his drinking and his personality problems. For example, he is seldom challenged and involved on the basis of his desire to be a good husband and father.

It has been my experience that many an alcoholic can be helped, particularly through family group therapy, to improve his relationships with people in his environment and that if these relationships are improved, even slightly, his motivation to stop drinking may be greatly enhanced. He may then begin to feel his family's efforts to understand and accept him before their hostility has driven him into almost complete isolation and further attempts at escape through alcohol.[1]

The fourth and perhaps the most important recommendation arising out of this study concerns the need for great attention to treatment of the children in the alcoholic's family.

In any troubled family that seeks help, the children may benefit indirectly as the parents are helped to adjust and mature. The children may also be helped if the family is responsive to family therapy. If, however, an alcoholic and his wife are highly resistant to treatment, their children are usually left to cope as best they can with continued alcoholism, disrupted family life, and their own conflicts and fears.

According to many therapists, all treatment of children should include treatment of the parents, since negative relationships and behavior on the part of adults almost invariably underlie the problems of children. There are, however, countless families affected by alcoholism in which this is not possible. In such instances I strongly believe that an attempt should be made to treat the children alone – preferably, of course, with the parents' consent. "The concept that children cannot be helped without their parents' involvement is a most dangerous misconception. If we do not help children whose parents will not co-operate, we are failing to treat 90 per cent of the children who have really severe problems."[2]

My own experience,*** as well as that of many psychiatrists and many other counsellors, has demonstrated that children *can* be helped to adjust to life with alcoholic parents and also to resolve or at least to handle some of their conflicts, fears, and hostilities. They may also be helped to acquire or regain a sense of trust in and love for other people and to develop some measure of self-awareness and self-esteem and a sense of security which will enable them to continue to grow. While they may not become as stable, perhaps,

***Since completing this study I have inaugurated a Youth Counselling Service in Metropolitan Toronto for children of alcoholic parents.

as they might have become had there been parental involvement, they may achieve a sufficient degree of security to face life successfully.

It must be recognized that treatment of adolescents requires rare skill. One researcher has suggested that many adults are afraid of adolescents and are therefore hostile to them.[3] If this is so, it is possible that many therapists unconsciously reject adolescents. Since most of the children I interviewed were adolescents, this might in part account for the fact that scarcely any had received direct help from any source.

The fifth recommendation is that more serious consideration should be given to the prevention of alcoholism and family breakdown.

It has been suggested that an attack on alcoholism at the grass-roots level might be undertaken by community agencies such as churches.

If the church would face the implications of the fact that the first six years of a person's life are the most important years from the standpoint of character structure and personality [it could] embark on a comprehensive program of parent education as a central focus of its work, making the discoveries of the psychologists concerning the emotional hungers of children ... easily available to all its parents. Through such a program, parents could come to see that healthy personality is "home-made" and that an ounce of mother is worth a pound of psychiatrist.... By helping parents to do that which they basically want to do but often cannot ... the church would help to prevent alcoholism ...[4]

If churches and other organizations worked cooperatively along these lines, it is within the realm of possibility that the tide of alcoholism might be stemmed. This would entail combined efforts on the part of all levels of government, alcoholism treatment centres, churches, public education, social agencies and individual citizens, as well as concentration on the subject of alcoholism in both undergraduate and graduate courses in medicine, nursing, social work, and pastoral theology.

The role of individuals in prevention also cannot be overemphasized. Every individual, lay or professional, has an opportunity and a responsibility to work toward change in public attitudes toward alcoholism and emotional disturbance. In a more enlightened community, those who are suffering from personality problems might not be as fearful of seeking help *before* becoming dependent on alcohol for a solution. Those who are already alcoholic would no longer be looked on as social lepers and as the sole responsibility of a handful of therapists. Individual citizens might also direct their attention to understanding the needs of the alcoholic's children and endeavor to bring appropriate pressure on the community to provide increased treatment resources for the family as well as treatment for some of these children.

I believe that we need more family life education centres, particularly for young couples; more appropriate community group activities for the whole family sponsored by the schools; more day-care centres for children who cannot be cared for by their parents for one reason or another; more unstructured drop-in centres where children might be involved in informal discussions of the problems they face. These are only a few of the ways in which an awakened community might help to improve family life and thus prevent development of patterns of dependence, irresponsibility, fear, and hopelessness and assist the children of alcoholic parents to find a healthy outlet for their frustrations and fears.

Expansion of services calls for more well-trained, involved therapists. Equally important is the need for a group of thoughtful, caring volunteer assistants who have not been unduly influenced by the kind of professionalism that seems to prevent many therapists from relating effectively to the alcoholic and his family. Such people might help us cope with professional shortages and might well make a vital contribution to the solution of this vast problem.

Because of the resistance of many alcoholics to becoming involved in treatment, and because many do respond to treatment when pressure to become involved is sufficient, I also feel that it is important to consider some form of compulsory treatment for the alcoholic and his family. While this would not prevent the onset of alcoholism, it might eliminate some of its worst manifestations – including heavy damage to family life.

By compulsory treatment, I do not mean sending a person to jail if he refuses treatment, but rather promoting a policy for business and industry in which employers would accept greater responsibility for helping their alcoholic employees. Such a policy might include referral of the employee for treatment, with leave of absence and the assurance that his position in the organization will be kept for him. Professional associations might be encouraged to bar alcoholic members from practice for a limited period in order to force them to face the problem.

Since alcoholism usually affects family life, similar authority and responsibility might be given to public health nurses, physicians, and teachers. These are the people who should be most aware of alcoholism in the family, and they are therefore appropriate persons to identify a family that may be in need of counselling and to report the fact to designated authorities. This is not entirely unprecedented, since family counselling is now recommended in Canada's new divorce laws. Even if the alcoholic did not take treatment, compulsory family counselling might force the spouse to take a serious look at her role in creating and maintaining the drinking problem. It would also enable her children to be reached for direct counselling, and this might help prevent the development of serious emotional problems as they grow into young adulthood.

I am acutely aware that this study leaves many questions unanswered. However, I hope that it may stimulate interest in more intensive research and that this book may draw increased attention to the need for treatment for children of alcoholic parents. If we consider some of the rights of children as outlined in the Children's Bill of Rights,[5] the importance of this stands out very sharply indeed.

For every child, understanding and the guarding of his personality as his most precious gift.

For every child, a home and that love and security which a home provides – an environment harmonious and enriching, free from conditions which tend to thwart his development.

For every child a community which recognizes and plans for his needs and protects him against physical danger, moral hazard and disease.

For every child such teaching and training as will prepare him for successful parenthood and, for parents, supplementary training to fit them to deal wisely with the problems of parenthood.

REFERENCES

1. CORK, R. M. Problem drinking and social workers. *Canadian Welfare*. 30 (5): 16–22, 1954.

   SAPIR, J. V. Social work and alcoholism. *Annals of the American Academy of Political and Social Science*. 315: 125–132, 1958.

2. SOL, G. New directions for school psychologists in big cities. Paper presented at the Annual Meeting of the Ontario Psychological Association, Toronto, 1967.

3. ODLUM, D. *Journey through Adolescence*. Baltimore: Penguin Books, 1963.

4. CLINEBELL, H. J. Jr. *Understanding and Counselling the Alcoholic*. New York: Abingdon Press, 1956.

5. White House Conference on Child Health and Protection, Washington, D.C., 1930.

Appendix

When I first contemplated making this study I took the view that a longitudinal approach would be essential. As plans progressed, however, it began to seem more important to take an immediate, if somewhat more hurried, look at whatever information might currently be gained simply from talking to children about their experiences, past and present, and not to concern myself with the follow-up aspect of the work. While a quick study would not provide us with the whole story of the problems that face thousands of children, I felt that it should surely constitute a basis for increased awareness and understanding of the nature of their suffering. It might also suggest ways of modifying some of our current methods of treating the alcoholic and enable us to make a start on the prevention of alcoholism and other ills in future generations. Moreover, such a study might produce hypotheses that could subsequently be tested by more rigorous methods.

Most studies of troubled children have been based on data obtained from their parents. Such information is often colored or distorted by the parents' own needs and attitudes. Because of the extreme defensiveness of both the alcoholic parent and his non-alcoholic spouse, I judged that it would be almost impossible to obtain from them a true picture of how their children were reacting to their home situations. It was this that first suggested the procedure of interviewing the children themselves – this plus the fact that my training and experience gave me the ability to reach out to these troubled children in a way that is often impossible for a pure scientist. Thus the data for this study were not obtained by means of psychological tests or questionnaires. These would have yielded useful statistics about the children but might not have given so much insight into their feelings or attitudes. Instead, I used the one-to-one interview which is so much a part of social casework and a frequently used device in social work research. By this means I hoped to gain a deeper understanding of the children and their life experiences.

The interviews with the children were informal, intimate, fairly unstructured, and more or less conversational. My participation consisted of helping the child to respond in his own way through general questions such as "Tell me about your father," or "How is school going?"

I was greatly helped in gaining the children's co-operation by four factors:

1) My past experience in working with children allowed me to approach them as people whose opinions I respected and needed.

2) I was able to obtain parental consent for the children to talk to me.

3) The children had a need and desire to talk freely about a subject that had long been taboo.

4) I was able to give the children the assurance of confidentiality. They were told that none of the information they revealed would be reported to their parents. (Their identities and those of their parents have, of course, been carefully disguised in this book.)

Because of the well-known defensiveness of alcoholics and their spouses, I had anticipated some resistance on the part of their children. To my surprise, even the few who initially seemed shy or hesitant began to talk freely once they sensed that the interviewer was interested in them and understood them. A few held back at first, particularly some of the ten-year-olds; but once started, they shared their feelings more than I had expected. The simplicity of the approach and the conversational nature of the interview seemed to win over even those who had initially expressed the feeling that they should not tell me certain things about their parents or about themselves. When it seemed important, I gave verbal recognition to their feelings by means of such remarks as, "I know it must be hard to talk about something that upsets you so much." At no time did I interject interpretations of their feelings or of the meaning of their parents' behavior. While I reacted with interest to everything the children said, I passed no judgment on how they felt or on their own or their parents' behavior. Occasionally, when a child was rather desperately asking for help, I referred to possibilities that were within his reach but refrained from dealing with his feelings. This was one of the most difficult aspects of the project from the standpoint of a treatment-oriented interviewer.

Interview Procedures

1) All children were seen by one interviewer, namely myself.
2) Interviews were usually held after school, in the early evening, or on weekends so as not to interfere with schooling or with parents' work schedules.
3) Parents or children, or both, were briefly welcomed in the waiting room. At this point I went over the procedures and stressed the confidentiality of the interview once more, so that parent and child heard these things together.
4) In instances where several brothers or sisters came together, I asked the children not to discuss their interviews with one another until all of them had been seen.
5) I interviewed each child alone in an office that was as unlike a business or professional setting as possible. It was furnished with comfortable, gaily

colored chairs, a rug, curtains, and pictures. The child and I sat in similar chairs with a low coffee table between us on which were an opened box of facial tissues and several small objects which the child could handle if he felt so inclined. The chairs were so placed that the child could see out of the window, and the room was large enough so that the child could walk around if he wished.

6) I gave each child a very brief, informal account of why I wanted to see him. I told him that I believed children saw, understood, and felt more about the problems than most parents realize, and that I believed that he and his parents would like to contribute to a study whose findings might lead people to help other children in similar circumstances. I assured the child that he could say as much or as little as he liked, and that whatever he told me would be helpful.

7) I recorded essential data such as age, school grade, position in the family, and age when the child was first aware of the alcohol problem.

8) I assured each child again that I would not report any of what he told me to his parents and that he did not need to tell his parents what he had told me unless he wanted to.

9) Each interview lasted approximately one-half to three-quarters of an hour. While it was as unstructured as possible, I directed the child, by means of a limited number of leading questions, to cover certain basic areas: relationships within and outside the family; interests; school work; attitudes to parental drinking; his own definition of alcoholism; his attitude to his mother's job, if she had

one; his attitude to his own possible future use of alcohol; quality of family life; which bothered him most, drinking or parental disharmony; and, lastly, whether he felt he had been affected by the home situation and, if so, in what ways.

10) With the child's permission, I made a shorthand verbatim recording of all that was said by both the child and myself.

Method of Obtaining Sample

Finding my sample was an arduous task which began in January, 1966, and took more than six months. The primary source was the patient files of the Alcoholism and Drug Addiction Research Foundation of Ontario.* Since the patient population of the A.R.F. is primarily from the middle or lower socio-economic group,** I also used the files of the Bell Clinic (now the Donwood Foundation)*** – which serves an upper socio-economic level – in order that I might obtain a more representative cross-section of children.

Two factors made it necessary to start with a fairly large basic sample of alcoholic patients. The first factor was that neither of these clinics kept any data on the presence of children in the alcoholic's family. The second was the well-known mobility of alcoholics,

---

*Essentially this is a public organization that provides treatment, research, and education in the field of alcoholism and other drug dependence in the province of Ontario.

**Defined on the basis of the father's occupation and education.

***The Donwood Foundation, in contrast to the A.R.F., is a private corporation operating a special hospital for patients suffering from alcoholism and other drug dependence. Regardless of which clinic their parents had attended, all children in the study were from the Metropolitan Toronto area.

which meant that a large proportion of patients would not be traceable. I therefore had lists made of all married patients who attended the clinics of the Alcoholism and Drug Addiction Research Foundation and the Donwood Foundation over a period of six years. The patients selected were between the ages of thirty-five and fifty, since I judged that these would be most likely to have children in the required age group.

From these two sources a basic sample of 3,813 patient files were available. Each one of these files – and they were frequently quite lengthy – had to be individually searched for the presence of children in the required age-group. In instances where such information was not found, the file was not removed from the sample until first-hand information was obtained from the parents themselves. After this review, some 2,808 files were discarded for one or more of the following reasons:

—patient's file contained no address;
—patient was found to be single;
—patient lived outside Metropolitan Toronto;
—patient had been separated from his children for more than five years;
—patient was married but had no children;
—patient was married but had no children in the required age-group;
—patient was found to be dependent on some substance other than alcohol;
—children were found to be permanent wards of the Children's Aid Society of Metropolitan Toronto or the Catholic Children's Aid Society of Metropolitan Toronto.

This left a total of 1,005 patients whom I could try to contact for permission to interview their children. Data regarding the patient's age, sex, marital status, number of children, employment, church affiliation, education, and the extent of treatment of both the alcoholic and his spouse were then recorded.

Following this, a letter was sent jointly to both the patient and his spouse, except in the case of separation, where it was sent to the parent with whom the children resided. No children were accepted for the study if their separation from the alcoholic parent was longer than five years or if the separation had occurred at an age when the children were too young for clear recall of their experiences while the alcoholic parent was in the home.

The letter to the patients of the two clinics identified me as a social worker who had been deeply interested in and concerned with alcoholism and the family for many years. It appealed for their help in a study vital to the understanding and treatment of alcoholism and its effects on family life. Enclosed in the letter was a self-addressed envelope and a form which asked the parents for the names and ages of their children and for written permission to have their children participate in a confidential interview. If permission was denied, the parents were asked to return the form and give their reasons for refusing. The following table indicates the response to these letters.

(A total of 62 sets of parents accepted the interview for their children, and 134 sets refused.)

Parents' Response to Letter

Letters sent	1,005
Returned unopened, unable to trace	375
Returned unopened, able to trace later and accepted	22
Returned unopened, able to trace later and refused	84
Not returned	362
Not returned, traced, but children not eligible	43
Returned and accepted	40
Returned and rejected (children not eligible)	29
Returned and refused	50

Procedure Followed after Parental Acceptance was Received

1) A telephone conversation was held with one or both parents. (On the average, five calls were made before an interview was finally held.) In two instances interviews were held with the parents before permission was given to see the children. These telephone conversations and contacts were intended to introduce the interviewer, interpret the study, allay fears (their own and the children's) regarding confidentiality, and gain parental co-operation in helping the child to participate. At the same time, there was emphasis on allowing the child himself to decide whether he was willing to be interviewed.

The calls were further designed to suggest that parents should not tell the child what to say or not to say, and that they should not question the child afterward about what happened. It was proposed, rather, that the child should be allowed to say whatever he wanted to.

Finally, the telephone calls were used to set a definite time for seeing the child and for gaining brief data from the parents about their family background.

2) A definite interview time was scheduled. It was found that an average of three appointments per child had to be set up because dates had to be changed owing to illness, school activities, and other factors.

3) If the alcoholic was currently in treatment, members of the appropriate clinical staff were contacted to let them know of the child's pending interview and to see if there was any reason, in their opinion, why the child should not be seen. Following the interview, a note was made in the patient's clinic file that the alcoholic's child or children had participated.

Organization of the Data

After completing my interviews with 115 children I spent several months reading and re-reading the thousands of words they had produced. During this period I developed a list of the areas touched on in the children's interviews. (See Form #1.) This list, which is a qualitative scale, served as a basis for evaluating each child's responses on a master chart (one which is too large to be reproduced here). This enabled me to see, more or less at a glance, any given child's total responses to the major aspects of his life situation.

Following this, I attempted to divide the children into groups according to the quality of their apparent relationships with both parents, the ways they seemed to have been affected, and the general reactions to family life they expressed. Thus, in a somewhat unscientific way, I arrived at a rough estimate of the degree of harm suffered by each child.

FORM #1

MAJOR AREAS TOUCHED ON IN INTERVIEWS

1. *Identifying Information*
   Christian Name
   Age at time of interview
   Age when first aware of problem
   Sex
2. Size of family (number of children)
   Position in family
3. School grade at time of interview

4. *Alcoholic Parent*
   Father
   Mother
   Both

5. *Status of Alcoholic Parent at Time of Interview*
   Sober, 1 year or more
   Drinking

6. *Treatment of Alcoholic Parent*
   1. None
   2. Family or pastoral counselling (3 months or more)
   3. Out-Patient (10 or more consecutive contacts)
   4. In-Patient (2–6 weeks in treatment centre)
   5. AA Group or Family Therapy (6 months or more)

7. *Treatment of Non-alcoholic Parent*
   1. None
   2. Family or pastoral counselling (3 months or more)
   3. Out-Patient (10 or more consecutive contacts)
   4. In-Patient (2–6 weeks in treatment centre)
   5. Alanon Group, wives or family group (6 months or more)

8. *Occupation of Father*
   1. Laboring
   2. Unskilled – Truck Driver, etc.
   3. Skilled – Mechanic, Brick Layer, Butcher, etc.
   4. White Collar – Sales, Clerical, etc.
   5. Proprietor (Owner)
   6. Free Lance – Writer, etc.
   7. Executive or Managerial
   8. Professional

9. *Education of Parents*
   1. Grade 8 or less
   2. Grade 9 to 13
   3. University – 2 years or graduation

10. *Church Affiliation*
    Regular church attendance of:
    1. Parents and children
    2. Non-alcoholic parent and children
    3. Alcoholic parent and children
    4. Non-alcoholic parent only
    5. Alcoholic parent only
    6. Children only
    7. No family members

11. *Child's View of Parental Relationship*
    1. Happy, enjoy each other, talk, do things together
    2. Happy, enjoy each other, etc., when no drinking
    3. Not happy, don't enjoy each other, etc., even when no drinking
    4. At odds – fighting, arguing – drinking or sober
    5. Separated – (literally or figuratively) each goes own way

12. *Child's View of Relationship with Alcoholic Parent*
    1. Enjoy each other, talks freely to, when no drinking
    2. Enjoy each other but can't talk to about things that matter – even when no drinking
    3. Rarely enjoys – often at odds with each other
    4. Parent rejects, dislikes – uninterested in child
    5. Parent dependent on child – to meet own needs
    6. Child over-identified with – too close to parent

13. *Child's View of Relationship with Non-alcoholic Parent*
    1. Enjoy each other, talks freely to when no fighting
    2. Enjoy each other but can't talk to about things that matter
    3. Rarely get along – at odds with each other most of time
    4. Parent rejects, dislikes, is not interested in child
    5. Parent dependent on child to meet own needs
    6. Child over-identified with parent

14. *Child's Reaction to Alcoholic's Drinking*
    1. OK to drink
    2. OK to drink a little, occasionally, but not to get drunk or fight
    3. OK to drink if non-drinking parent wouldn't get so upset
    4. Understands why drinking parent has to drink – feels sorry for
    5. Frightened of parent when drinking

15. *Non-alcoholic Parent's Reaction to Partner's Drinking*
    1. OK to drink
    2. OK to drink a little, occasionally, but not to get drunk or fight
    3. Fears drinking may cause accidents or fire
    4. Angry, hurt by consequences (debts, non-support, abuse) rejection, etc.
    5. Against drinking by women – mothers – wives
    6. Against drinking by men – fathers – husbands
    7. Against any drinking – hates it

16. *Focus of Child's Concern*
    1. The drinking
    2. The drunkenness
    3. Parental quarrelling or fighting
    4. Unhappiness between parents – (hurt and hate)
    5. Drinking parent's lack of interest in
    6. Non-drinking parent's lack of interest in

17. *Child's Definition of Alcoholism*
    1. Person who drinks too much – drinks constantly
    2. Person who *has* to drink to escape, can't stop
    3. Person who is stupid, selfish, not grown up
    4. Person who is worried, unhappy, sick, afraid of life
    5. Something that's a waste of money
    6. Something that's a bad habit
    7. Something that makes you a different person
    8. Something that destroys or ruins a person

18. *Child's View of Problems Caused by Drinking*
    1. No particular problems
    2. Money problems
    3. Unduly upsets other parent
    4. Parents behave inconsistently, unpredictably
    5. People don't like you – you feel different – pity you – make fun of you
    6. Physical abuse between parents – alcoholic destructive
    7. Accidents to alcoholic parent – or jail
    8. Loss of respect for alcoholic parent – ashamed of
    9. Destroys alcoholic parent or family

19. *Child's View of Alcoholic Parent as a Parent*
    1. Good parent (like any other parent)
    2. Good parent, etc., except when drinking
    3. Good parent, etc., except when fighting
    4. Not so good – selfish – self-centered
    5. Not good – feels parent doesn't care, doesn't understand you
    6. Not good – doesn't behave like other parents

20. *Child's View of Non-alcoholic Parent as a Parent*
    1. Good parent (like any other parent)
    2. Good parent, etc., except when affected by other parent's drinking
    3. Good parent, etc., except when fighting
    4. Not so good – selfish – self-centered
    5. Not so good – feels parent doesn't care, doesn't understand you
    6. Not good – doesn't behave like other parents

21. *Child's Relationship with Siblings, Peers, Other Adults*
    1. Close to one or more of them, does things with, talks with
    2. Reasonably close, etc., does things with – but can't talk to
    3. Not close, fights with, at odds most of time
    4. Not close, feels can't be trusted – wouldn't understand
    5. Doesn't have any real friends
    6. Doesn't know any adults to talk to – can't talk to anyone

22. *Child's Attitude to Mother's Working*
    1. More money for debts, material things
    2. Mother less tense, worried; more peaceful
    3. Dislikes – misses mother
    4. Dislikes – afraid to be alone with drinking parent
    5. Dislikes – as has too much responsibility for household tasks
    6. Dislikes – as mother overworked – always tired
    7. Resents – feels father should support
    8. Doesn't care – mother's absence not important

23. *Child's Attitude to Own Future Use of Alcohol*
    1. May drink at parties or special occasions
    2. May drink, but not like drinking parent does
    3. Won't drink, stupid, disgusting to – don't like taste of it
    4. Won't drink, waste of money
    5. Won't drink, afraid of getting like parent
    6. Won't drink, upsets family life
    7. Won't drink, not healthy, wrong to drink, hurts other people
    8. Won't drink, women shouldn't drink
    9. Won't drink, no one should drink
    10. Drinking now

24. *Child's View of the Ways he has been Affected*
    1. Not affected
    2. School work affected
    3. Relationships within family affected
    4. Relationships outside of family affected
    5. Physical health suffered
    6. Worries constantly about not being liked by peers
    7. Worries constantly about being different
    8. Has overall sense of anxiety and fear of future
    9. Feels burdened by too much responsibility – has had to grow up too fast
    10. Is constantly ashamed, feels hurt, gets upset, and cries readily
    11. Is never sure of self, lacks self-confidence
    12. Feels unwanted by one or both parents
    13. Is constantly angry, hostile toward parents
    14. Is overly self-reliant, feels unable to trust or depend on anyone

15. Feels uncomfortable with or fearful of the opposite sex
16. Is constantly defiant, at odds with authority
17. Feels hopeless and depressed, lacks ambition, but passively accepts situation
18. Thinks constantly of escaping from family or from responsibilities generally

25. *Child's Present View of Family Life*
    1. Normal (like – as good as – other families)
    2. Normal (like – etc.) when no drinking
    3. Normal (like – etc.) when no fighting
    4. Abnormal (not like, not as good as other families)
    5. Abnormal – father absent or not like other fathers
    6. Abnormal – mother absent or not like other mothers

26. *Child's Feeling About Future*
    1. OK as it is
    2. Hopeful (change will come or has come)
    3. Not hopeful, feels it won't ever change
    4. Not hopeful, feels caught, powerless to do anything
    5. Hopeless, doesn't feel a part of family
    6. Hopeless, doesn't need a family

27. *Interviewer's Assessment of Damage to Child*
    1. None
    2. Slight – will likely be resolved (or has been)
    3. Fairly serious – but could still respond to change and help
    4. Very serious – likely lasting without intensive therapy